Darling,
Love
Me
Into
Submission

**A Humbling Experience of
Love, Respect, and Honor!**

Prophetess Betty Samuels Moore

xulon
PRESS

Darling, Love Me Into Submission:
A Humbling Experience of
Love, Respect, and Honor

by

Prophetess Betty Samuels Moore

Dedication

$\mathscr{I}$ dedicate this book to my husband, Bishop H. Clenton Moore, for being the most supportive man in the world. Darling, I humbly submit to you. You found me at a time in my life when I was polluted with past issues, yet you saw me in my future, cleansed with integrity and openness. I adore you; you singled me out from the rest, washed me, clothed me, and adorned me with precious ornaments. I long to give you my love and my years.

Ann Latimer, my dearest friend, encouraged me twenty-five years ago to marry this awesome man, whom I had not known very long. Thank you, friend.

Shortly after we met in February of 1981, I served as the Student Government Association President with Florida Community College. One of our assignments was to have a black history program. Our speaker was Reverend Martin Luther King, Sr. As we were escorted from the airport, Reverend King asked if I were married. I responded no, but I was engaged. He asked to meet the man to whom I was engaged. That evening they met, and Reverend King inspired wisdom in my heart as he spoke these words to Herb. He said, "You need to marry her. Don't let her go; she is a good woman." He advised him to marry me. From our brief encounter, he knew I was a good woman. To Daddy King, thank you for seeing the goodness of God abiding in me. In Christ, we shall meet again.

Honey, we have been through Hades, but now we are eating the good of the land. I express gratitude for finding me, your gift, offered to you by God. You married me when it was revealed in your spirit that I was your good thing. Forevermore I will crack your toes as you rock my world. Thank you for your prayers, patience, and support.

Acknowledgments

I thank God for giving me wisdom in my life as well as vision and insight to pen on paper what was in my heart. People have told me on many occasions that I was a late bloomer. No, I am not a late bloomer; I have come into my own. I am walking in my season. Now is the time for me to emerge from the back side of the mountain and come forth as pure gold.

Some of the warmest things that ever happened to me were the words of encouragement from my family, who told me to write the book and keep it real.

Special thanks to my pastors and spiritual leaders, Apostles T. C. & A. R. Maxwell of P.R.O.C.L.A.I.M. Worldwide Ministries, Atlanta, Georgia. They enlightened me with their good judgment and insight. Along with them, Sister Patricia Roberson, Pastors Adrin and Monique Washington, Pastor Dorothy Jackson, Elder Tarra Jones, and the membership of Temple Of Light, you were the first to sow into the vision. Thank you kindly. I am appreciative of your prayers and the powerful thoughts of how to make this book successful. Day after day you boosted my spirit to take time to hear from God, making sure this was what God wanted for His people's eyes and ears.

Contents

Introduction

On May 28, 2000, following the christening ceremony of my grand niece, Kennedi, the family gathered in the home of my sister-in-law for dinner. While waiting for the preparation of the meal, I overheard the young adults conversing. They chatted about their lives: the good and the not so good. From their lips, I sensed a feeling of desperation in their voices which sighed, "Help me. I'm falling. I need clarity."

As a woman of God, I took a seat to judge the quality of their conversation. I listened attentively without imposing my spiritual viewpoint, but to understand clearly and get a grip on their conversation. I listened for approximately thirty minutes, and God knows I wanted to speak. Because I wasn't asked, I made the conscious decision not to interfere. It was hard and difficult, but my youngest son Vincent and my eldest nephew Uzair were there to aid me in that process. Approximately forty-five minutes into the conversation, my nephew Darius's darling wife Sonya asked me a question concerning submission. She asked, "Why are women discussing submission? In Atlanta, at a Women's Conference, speakers are encouraging women to submit. I think they should divide single women from married women while discussing such issues. Aunt Betty, how do you define submission?"

There it was, an opportunity for me to speak. I was searching for words, trying my best to get a feel of the word and not to be offensive, but I couldn't speak. Soon I verbalized, "Submission is a state of humbling yourself. It's a humbling experience where you honor and reverence your husband." Before I could finish answering the question, my niece Wallene, Kennedi's mother, interjected, "Submission is respecting your spouse in a humble manner. It has to do with love and respect, and as Aunt Betty said, it is to humble yourself."

In retrospect, I can say to the women of this world that submission is the process of eliminating pride and taking on the spirit of humility. It is an act of surrendering without thinking about the consequences, especially when it comes to God. We must do what his Word says and not analyze it. Submission is about being under the authority of God with the person you love.

Men and women should submit for the purpose of being obedient to God. For "He has put all things under His feet." But when He says "all things are put under Him," it is evident that He who put all things under Him is excepted. Now when all things are made subject to Him, then the Son Himself will also be subject to Him who put all things under Him, that God may be all in all.

1 Corinthians 15:27-28 NKJV

From that position, I was inspired to write this book. There is a great deal of helpful information on the market concerning submission. Then why write another book, you ask? It's like a preacher ministering the same sermon weekly although the congregation is tired of hearing it. Eventually, one brave member asks the question, "Pastor, why the same sermon every week?"

His response is, "The Lord knows that you have not gotten it yet, and He wants me to preach the same sermon until you get it in your heart, soul, mind, and spirit." I truly believe this is why God led me to write this concerning this complicated subject. Many people can intellectualize submission, yet they don't have it in their heart, soul, mind, and spirit to actually submit one to another.

My purpose for writing this book is also to encourage men and women to submit under the authority of a true and living God.

It is not difficult to submit when hearts are right before God. But it is difficult to humble before others if there is a spirit of refusal to change, to bow down, or a spirit of stubbornness and rebellion residing in our hearts.

The Bible teaches us to humble ourselves in the sight of the Lord, and He will lift us up and make our lives significant. As we humble ourselves, we are demonstrating the same compassion that Christ has for God. He submitted Himself to the authority of His Father.

My nephew and his wife have had many difficult days, but she has a submissive attitude towards him. She is open-minded in a loving way where he is rocking her world because of the softness of her speech and mannerism. She learned that a soft answer turns away wrath: but grievous words stir up anger (Proverbs 15:1). Together, they are happier, healthier, wealthier, and established.

Betty Samuels-Moore

Part One

Your Love Is Ever Before Me

As the evening breaks, I long for the gentle, sweet touch of your lips. Kiss me with the kisses from your heart, revealing without a spoken word that you are happy to be my man.

You are my man who listens with the ear of attentiveness and judges not my motive, but understands my mind.

Darling, I love you more and more each day for having an understanding heart. You have proven in so many ways that your love is strong and powerful.

When you could have given up on me, you maintain to provide for your darling wife.

My sweetness, your love is ever before me. Thank you for calling me your darling wife, whom you have loved into submission!

CHAPTER 1

Just for You!

And thou shalt love the LORD thy God with all thine heart, and with all thy soul, and with all thy might.

Deuteronomy 6:5

Wherefore they are no more twain, but one flesh. What therefore God hath joined together, let not man put asunder.

Matthew 19:6

How breathtaking it was seeing Sheldon and Linda join hands that raining day in October to receive their wedding vows. They met two years prior to getting married. Ultimately, in love were they. She submitted to him earlier in this relationship. Whatever he wanted, she was there to provide. Each protected the other. They opened the door of vulnerability, having freedom to communicate openly without the fear of their past experiences returning to hurt them in their future.

Earlier in the day, some felt there wasn't going to be a wedding. It had been drizzling all day, but a few hours before the wedding the mild rain escalated to a hurricane. Many who were to come couldn't for the harsh winds and rain. But those who made it, including me, the groom's mother, were an hour late. I wasn't trying to be fashionably late, I was late as the result of the fierce rain. My yard was flooded, and water was up to my front door. I concentrated on the Word and prayed purposefully for the rain to end and water to rescind. I could not miss my son's wedding. God heard my prayer. The water rescinded, and I was able to walk in the water, getting my shoes wet. Many knew that I loved the couple when they saw my $200 shoes wet. To me, beautiful are the feet of those who wear dazzling, expensive shoes. That's me; I was the one with the beautiful, wet shoes who saved the wedding.

While driving, water got in the car. The bottom of my fuchsia dress was dipping in water and my bow, which wasn't attached securely, came off the dress. I was a mess. With fortitude, I pressed my way, praying that the car wouldn't stop. Finally, I made it there. It wasn't about me; it was about the bride and the groom.

After my arrival, I had to walk down the aisle, discreetly holding the bow that was no longer attached to the dress. I performed smartly and eloquently, as I moved swiftly down the aisle to meet my husband. No longer did I mind being wet. I was going to meet my king, my lover, and my friend. For a moment, I thought I was the bride. Quickly I came to my senses and rushed to be with my husband.

Everyone anticipated seeing the bride. Seeing the bride walk down the aisle is the high point of any wedding.

Despite all the accurate planning, chances are that something unexpected will happen on that special day. It could have been that the best man wouldn't come, the bridesmaids' dresses would be too small, or the caterer wouldn't show with the food already prepared. Someone might be pulled from the audience to assist with preparing the food or frosting the cake.

On their day, rain was a hindrance for an hour. Although we were late, seeing her march down the aisle softly touching her godfather's hand, as he carried her to embrace her father, was an amazing sparkle to the audience. Her father stood as if he were a royal guard, waiting for the queen's entrance. Truly, she was a queen, draped in a contemporary, lacy, white dress, which flattered her figure.

As she approached her father, he turned towards her and extended his arm. As she made that last step to reach her father, there was a glow that brightened the room as she moved her eyes to look upon the man who chose her to be his bride. That moment was worth the wait. In a twinkle of an eye, she was to be taken from the safety of her father to her king.

The look upon their faces demonstrated the kind of love that God has for us. It is a love so deep, for it is unconditional. Their eyes pictured that no matter what, their love would shatter any obstacle, problems, or differences they may encounter.

Then, the reason for our presence began. Marriage is a serious union. When a man makes that decision to take on the responsibility of another person, he has truly invested time and received spiritual counseling, knowing the full realization of his commitment, responsibility, and dedication to his wife.

A woman sees herself adorned to meet her husband's needs and to be his help meet. Her obligation is to help him. She encourages her man, and nurtures him in the midst of his overwhelming new dimension of accountabilities.

Linda's pastor asked, "Who gives this bride to be married?"

Her father stated, "I do." Before he could complete those words, Sheldon had already reached for his bride. He took his bride and stepped forward towards the pastor.

To the groom the pastor said, "Sheldon, do you take Linda as your wife, to love her as Christ loves the church, to protect her and care for her until death do you part? Do you promise to love, honor, and respect her as your wife?"

The groom responded, "I do." He turned to Linda and said, "I have chosen to leave my father and mother and to cling to you, to be your husband from this very moment."

The audience was sobbing cheerfully with acceptance. The pastor turned to Linda and said, "Do you take Sheldon as your husband, to submit to him and reverence him as the head of the house? Do you commit to him as being first in your heart above all, except the Father which is in heaven?"

Softly Linda spoke, "I do." She turned towards her husband and spoke. "I submit to you. I promise to be your wife and to love you from this day forward."

The groom, with tears in his eyes, gave her a small grin, which perhaps meant, "I know you love me." The ceremony of marriage continued with them placing rings on each other's fingers and repeating separately, "With this ring, I pledge my heart to you, to love you forever and never take advantage of that love." Together they repeated, "These rings are an indication of our faith and fidelity." Their confessions were sealed with prayer. They kissed, jumped over the broom holding hands, and left the church to serve one another for the rest of their lives.

HIS MAJESTIC LOVE

God's love for mankind is wonderful! His magnificent love reigns from heaven to earth. His love is sovereign and majestic. Our sovereign God moves throughout the universe, demonstrating his love to all who accept him as Lord and Savior.

From the bottom of my heart, I humbly admit that I love the Lord. He is my great king, my peace and my fortress! He saved me from hell and damnation. He saw me polluted in my own blood and said unto me, "Live." Therefore, I salute Him with love and kisses. I kiss Him with kisses of my mouth as I praise and glorify His awesome name.

King Solomon put in songs, many years ago, "Kiss me with the kisses of your mouth: for your love is better than wine. Draw me; I will be glad and will rejoice in you; I will remember your love more than wine: the upright loves you" (Song of Solomon 1:2, 4).

What an awesome expression unto the Lord! You too, can join in, singing a love song, telling Him that you are grateful to Him. He created us for His glory. In an eloquent manner, join voices unto the Lord of His greatness and His majestic love.

Throughout the United States, in a Sunday morning worship service, there isn't a time when believers do not assemble together and echo these thoughts: "I love you, Lord, today like never before. I love you with my whole heart, mind, and soul. I worship you and adore you. You have been so good to me, and I come to praise Your glorious name."

The Lord must be ecstatic that there are groups of people from every socio-economic level, with clean hearts, who congregate for one purpose: to demonstrate their love towards Him through worship in spirit and in truth.

My belief is that when we praise God it is a celebration of His creation, works, and benefits. King David mentions in Psalm 103:2 that we should "Bless the LORD at all times, and forget not all his benefits."

I feel we should honor and bless the Lord with ever fiber of our being, showing that we have a heart of appreciation for what he has done for us.

He wants our praise and worship. Beyond that, He wants them to be compacted in truth. He inhabits the praises of His people.

As the body of Christ, it should be a privilege to praise Him for who He is and for what His name represents. God is powerful, majestic, glorious, wonderful, and mighty. Isaiah 9:6 describes God as wonderful, counselor, the mighty God, the everlasting Father, the Prince of Peace.

Let everything that has breath praise Him at all times. He is worth the glory, honor, and praise. In John 1:3 we read, "Through him all things were made; without him nothing was made that has been made." Colossians 1:16-17 makes a parallel declaration: "For by him all things were created: things in heaven and on earth, visible and invisible, whether thrones or powers or rulers or authorities; all things were created by him and for him. He is before all things, and in him all things hold together."

Most importantly, God is worthy of our praise. In 2 Samuel 22:4, these words must inspire us: "I will call on the LORD, who is worthy to be praised: so shall I be saved from mine enemies." 1 Chronicles 16:25 says, "For great is the LORD and greatly to be praised: he also is to be feared [honored] above all gods."

In Psalm 48:1, David speaks. "Great is the LORD, and greatly to be praised in the city of our God, in the mountain of his holiness."

Praising God sets the tone for quality time with Him. Praising his name reminds us of His identity and reinforces our understanding of who He is.

The evidence of praising God is that we can see our own sin. We are quickly led into confession of our sins, which in turn leads us to praising and thanking God for His mercy, grace, and forgiveness. Praising God changes the atmosphere to work for our good. When obstacles are against us, a silent cry or a loud voice with a sincere heart will change the heart of God.

In Isaiah 38:1-5 the prophet Isaiah told Hezekiah, who was sick unto death, that he would die and not live. "Then Hezekiah turned his face toward the wall and prayed unto the LORD, And said, Remember now, O LORD, I beseech thee, how I have walked before thee in truth and with a perfect heart, and have done that which is good in thy sight. And Hezekiah wept sore. Then came the word of the LORD to Isaiah, saying, Go, and say to Hezekiah, Thus saith the LORD, the God of David thy father, I have heard thy prayer, I have seen thy tears: behold, I will add unto thy days fifteen years." Hezekiah reminded God of his faithful praise, and God honored him by prolonging his life.

We all need something extended in our lives. What an opportunity to sacrifice ourselves and magnify the Lord's holy and righteous name!

The authority and power of Christ are unique. Although Hezekiah was sick unto death, God reversed his words, and he recovered from his sickness (v.9).

In Hebrews 1:3 we find these words, "Who being the brightness of [his] glory, and the express image of his person, and upholding all things by the word of his power, when he had by himself purged our sins, sat down on the right hand of the Majesty on high."

If we think about this, there is power in His name and in the word of God. In the midst of spiritual death and throbbing pains, we should give a shout unto Him. While we're in great pain, adore Him. It's hard, but press and do it. He is worth us forgetting about ourselves.

God has good things for His children, and His healing bread is one of those good things that He has provided for His children, according to Mark 7:27. And in Psalm 91:16, the writer speaks. "With long life I will satisfy him, and show him my salvation."

I recall one encounter with God's healing power concerning a simple headache. When there is a painful headache, one does not feel like doing anything, especially praising God. If we are not mature in God, we will give in to the headache or any other condition. That is how I felt twenty-six years ago, until I entered His presence and knew the value of praise and worship. On this particular day in 1980, I was getting ready to exit the church doors when a young man stopped me for prayer. He said, "Evangelist Samuels, will you pray for my headache?"

My response was, "Son, my head is hurting. I need someone to pray for me."

Just before I reached him, my head began to ache. Prior to that point of entrance, my head wasn't hurting. At that moment, God convicted me. God knows how to get our attention. He said to me, "If you pray for him, your headache will be gone before your prayer is ended."

I began to pray for the young man, and in the midst of praying for him, the Lord healed me! At what point He healed me, I don't recall. However, when the prayer was completed, my head wasn't hurting.

I praised God for demonstrating to me that if I forget about me and pray for someone else, my healing, which is already there, will manifest. I've learned to give thanks and praise in all things. I didn't only praise God because He healed me; I praised Him because of the revelation of who He is. Too, I observed through that experience that I would be able to sense other people's conditions, and at that point I must pray for them, requested or not. My ministry was to intercede for others, to act on somebody else's behalf, and to do unto others as I wanted them to do unto me. Through God's love and my obedience, we both were healed.

THIS SHALL REMAIN IN YOUR HEART

Love is the utmost attribute of God. From the beginning God loved us. He created man in His image. That's love! In the image of God he created him: male and female. After man's creation, He blessed them and told them to be fruitful and multiply, to fill the earth and subdue it (Genesis 1:27-28). That's love! Because of God's love, we should love Him with all our heart, with all our soul, with all our strength, and with our entire mind (Luke 10:27).

Even though we love the Lord, we need to know that we are loved by Him at all times. We know that He is with us. Christ tells us in Matthew 28:20b, "I am with you always, even unto the end of the world."

You may ask, "Does He love me? I have gone through so much in life; does He really love me?" He does. Christ died for us. He knew no sin, and He died that we may live and have eternal life (John 3:15). Most Christians know that God loves them, but their lack of understanding of His love may be contributed to things. They may attribute God's love to giving them "things."

Daily He gives us new mercies and grace. He gave his Son, and Christ gave His life for us. He became sin for us. My goodness, that's love! I thank him for goodness and mercy. Psalm 23:6 states that, "Surely goodness and mercy shall follow me all the days of my life: and I will dwell in the house of the LORD forever." To me, it sounds like I should give Him glory and praise because they will follow me to watch over me, protect me, and shield me.

THE "I AM" OF GOD

We, as a people, don't always feel loved, especially when we are looking for things and not the "I Am" of God. The God we serve, who is "I Am Love, I Am Peace, I Am Prosperity, I Am Healer, and I Am More than Enough," is accessible to us, and He loves us unconditionally.

But the natural man, the one you really want to love you, doesn't, although his love is not questioned, for he gives you things.

Yet, when he does love, his love is based on conditions. I love you because of your smile, your beautiful brown eyes, your legs, what you do for me. Without you, I'll be nothing.

Why can't love simply be, "I love you without demands? Love me for who I am, and not for what you think I have or what I can do for you?"

Unfortunately, you lose when you see God as being represented by things. You look for things in God and look for things in a relationship as the ultimate sign for love.

No wonder various women don't have a natural man or have an intimate relationship with God, because they want things. There is nothing wrong with wanting things, but you need to seek God.

In Isaiah 43:1-4, the prophet Isaiah writes this message, "But now thus saith the LORD that created thee, O Jacob, and he that formed thee, O Israel, Fear not: for I have redeemed thee, I have called thee by thy name; thou art mine. When thou passest through the waters, I will be with thee; and through the rivers, they shall not overflow thee: when thou walkest through the fire, thou shalt not be burned; neither shall the flame kindle upon thee. Since thou wast precious in my sight, thou hast been honorable, and I have loved thee: therefore will I give men for thee, and people for thy life."

God demonstrated His love in an unconditional manner. He created and formed you. For that reason, you should not be fearful for any cause. He redeemed (emancipated, freed, and bought) you; you are His. Wherever the situation or circumstance is, as you pass by it He is with you. The situation may be water and the circumstance may be fire. Fear not! The waters will not overflow you. The fire shall not burn you, and the flames will not ignite upon you. He does this because you are precious in His sight; you have been honorable and he loves you. Therefore, He gave Himself for you, and people for your life. When you should have been dead, persecuted, and lost all that you had, He gave others for your life. The "I AM" should be praised and honored at all times.

As a rule, some want God and that significant person to prove love through things. Sometimes, you will never see love through the eye of the spirit or the heart of God because you are consumed by things.

Suppose you are given things, but the person who gives you things doesn't love you. Can you still love him or her even though he does not want to be intimate with you? It's obvious that you want the one you love to love you, but he or she doesn't always.

And that's not a good feeling, loving someone who doesn't love you. In your mind, you sometimes think that time or age is a contributing factor to determine if you love or whether you are going to be loved.

That person who you want to love you could be in love with somebody else, and your waiting might be in vain. The love he or she has for you could be the love of friendship, and sometimes you want more. Yet, when there is nothing more, can you accept the fact that he or she doesn't care for you in the same way?

He or she not loving you doesn't make you a bad person. It means he or she didn't love you. Love is for you, and a wonderful person is coming into your life. In the meantime, can you walk in the love called "agape?" Agape is the God kind of love, loving someone in a godly manner.

You know the old saying, "You can't get blood from a turnip." This may not set firm in your spirit, but this is truth.

You are at a point in your lives when you don't need to waste energy praying for the heart of another person, when they aren't interested in you. You said God told you that he was your husband. Your husband has walked away from the relationship. He expressed that he didn't love you and needed space. Give him all the space he needs. If he is your husband, pray and move forward.

Edna was a person like that. She loved Sylvester and wanted to marry him. Without doubt, she knew he was her husband. They dated for years. She ran to many spiritual leaders to have them pray that he would marry her. He had other women, but she was determined to wait for him. "One day, he will marry me," she said. He did! When he couldn't perform sexually and the doctor diagnosed him with cancer and other medical problems, he wanted her. They married, and for many years she served him from his sick bed. While in the shopping mall, we met, and I asked about her family. I did not know that they had married, and that he had died, leaving her with a house and his retirement.

She wasted energy for an old house which needed much repair, his name, and a retirement check about which she was complaining. Why make the ultimate sacrifice only to complain about your decision, when you had an open door to leave? She couldn't leave because she wanted things. Too, she wanted to show the other women that he was her man. Edna was holding on to an image, a picture she organized through her imagination.

Imagine this: you have known men who liked you and gave you things, and it wasn't a requirement to be intimate with them. And they didn't desire to be intimate with you. Perhaps they gave to you because they felt sadness in their hearts. There you were, separated from your husband, providing for three sons, going to school, and working part time, trying to make ends meet.

The bottom line was, they cared only in a friendly way. Even if you wanted more, they treated you as a little sister or as a daughter.

You weren't offended, and you didn't push to get more. You were content. In your heart, you knew there were no more for them to give beyond the car payments, children's school tuition, jewelry, clothes, and shoes. They were on assignment to help you with things for a season. You didn't ask for things, but things were given that they knew you needed. Don't waste time on things; spend time in prayer for godly possessions.

WHEN OUR HEARTS ARE IN RIGHT STANDING

We should be grateful and highly stimulated that we are able to generate love to God and our fellow man. As we go after the heart of Christ, things will come automatically.

The "I Am" is obligated to provide for His children. When your hearts are in right standing, He is obligated to bring you into the presence of those persons who are essential to your success in life.

Those individuals assisted you until God released them. They were on assignment from God and for the benefit of those who think you used them. Not so, you did not use them. You had nothing to do with their giving. God will open the flood gates of blessings for His children.

29

Too, you didn't have to hide behind the bush, trading car seats – moving from one car to another, sneaking a little kiss, or letting them touch you. They invested in a dedicated woman who had a need. Their motives were pure, and they received godly benefits on their return. They were not after your body; they walked in obedience to God. He does have people on assignments to help you. Get your heart right to receive what He has for you.

FROM THE HEART MY MOUTH SPEAKS

From the perception of a tightfisted heart, it is difficult to conceive that someone is willing to sow into their life with a pure motive. Giving doesn't come easy for some. You know, too, love doesn't come easy for them.

Through the years, many men and women have been hurt, and they don't want to give to another person from the pureness of their hearts. As a result, it is simply easy for some men and women to turn love on like a water faucet. That type is easy to fall in love, and they use the faucet as toughness. You'll hear them say, "My love is on convenience. I don't trust you; I don't know you. If you can't do for me or provide for me, my love is dissolved." Usually, they are playing a game of toughness.

Then again, there are scores of hurting women who have vowed never to love because of the severity of past hurts and pains. Love affairs and friendships have turned into hateful relationships because of unresolved issues and challenges.

Unfortunately, there are countless Christian men and women who are included in this predicament. All Christians are called to love their neighbors and their brothers, but also to love their enemies (Matthew 5:44). Yet, when hurt is alive, it becomes difficult to love those who have hurt us.

But it is written in John 13:34-35, that a new commandment is given to counteract what we find difficult. It is written, "A new commandment I give unto you, that ye love one another; as I have loved you, that ye also love one another. By this shall all men know that ye are my disciples, if ye have love one to another."

The determining factor whether you can love is by your acceptance of God's love through His Son, Christ Jesus our Savior.

From the heart my mouth speaks to men who are fearful of falling in love. Fear is not an option when you know for certain that you aren't to get involved with a woman unless you are serious about her welfare and feel strongly that you can fall in love with her.

For the most part, men have the tendency to confuse "love" with "lust." They lust after a woman for what she can do for them; they want to sleep with her before they get to know her heart, soul, and spirit. I might be wrong, but I feel that a man can sleep with one woman and have his heart in bed with another woman due to fear of commitment.

You must be thinking, "He bumped his cranium." He did, but not over you. Sad to say, love has nothing to do with him being sexually satisfied. At that moment, it's all emotional. While he is getting what he wants, he may say, "Baby, I love you." Meaning, I love what you are doing and giving me. He doesn't know you; he met you last night. If you want to be meticulous, it could have been last week. Wake up, you are sleeping too long. He is still operating out of lust.

Lust for a man can mean the heat of passion. Don't be confused; that's not love. That's called the stick shift maneuver. True love is when he is trying to enjoy intimacy with you: getting to know you, your heart, and your thoughts. It is not being eager to bear down on your body.

True love does not love only in speech, articulating words to satisfy the flesh. But true love is to love in deed [action] and in truth [certainty] (1 John 3:18). We see love differently from God. The Lord said to Samuel, "Look not on his countenance, or on the height of his stature; because I have refused him: for the LORD seeth not as man seeth; for man looketh on the outward appearance, but the LORD looketh on the heart." (1 Samuel 16:7)

That which we think we need, we don't need. When a woman says she's hungry, she could be dehydrated. Fluids are needed to satisfy the body, not always food. When you feel you are in love, for the most part, it could be lust of the eye, wanting fulfillment of the flesh.

CHAPTER 2

The "Love Me" Game

❋

As a young girl, perhaps like most young girls of today, you were in and out of love without having a boyfriend. You created in your mind the boys you wanted to love. To some, it sounds silly that a girl would think of doing something like this. Well, believe it; it does happen. In fact, some used to pick yellow daisies for playing the "love me" game. They repeated, "He loves me; he loves me not."

As they pulled off each leaf, most of the time repeating "he loves me" didn't reach a boy that they really wanted to love them, so they purposed in their hearts to cheat to make those words fit. They never wanted to be unloved. Sometimes, it didn't work out that way, and they had to eliminate a few names by prioritizing who they wanted to love them more.

The end result of the game was not favorable; it didn't matter how much you tried to manipulate "he loves me" by pretending that you forgot to say, "He loves me." It didn't always work for your good, but you knew you had the ability to make things be what you wanted by cheating and manipulation. With the power and control of the pen, you scratched out or marked through a name and got what you wanted. On the inside you didn't feel good, for your decision wasn't genuinely honest.

At an early age, a few of my sisters found out that cheating didn't work for them, and manipulation should not be a part of their character. Those women can't speak for you, but every time they had the urge to manipulate things into being, they remembered that they would get caught, and quickly changed their minds. It is important that you bring the message home, to all your relatives, and do as my relatives told me: keep it real.

Some things are not in the divine will of God. You can't make anything fit. Permissive will occurs when one insists on having it his way. Our will is not God's perfect will for our lives.

CALL THINGS INTO EXISTENCE

One summer evening in July 2001, my husband and I were summoned to the home of a young couple, Clara and James Martin, who were having marital problems. They had been married for eight years and had one daughter. Clara wanted to have another child, but James was doubtful of becoming a father again. That created many sleepless nights of arguments and complaints.

Our purpose was to defuse the situation. My husband began by asking James how they met. What attracted her to him? With gladness in his eyes the young man said, "I snake charmed her."

That blew my mind. I sat with my mouth open, wanting to hear how he had charmed her. My husband was cool. He looked at James and said, "Continue, please."

He told us, "In school, I had enough trust in myself that when I saw her, she would be mine. I snake charmed her. It didn't matter how long it took, she would not resist my charm. I ran behind her, even after I graduated from high school. She attempted to run but not far. At the right moment, she fell into my arms, and we married."

Ironically, he called things into existence. He did whatever he had to get her, and after he had her, he didn't want to do what was necessary or meaningful to keep her. He wanted her back then, but now he doesn't want to give her what she wants. She only wants to live in his presence. Whatever it takes, he should be willing to do it, because he wanted her love. Whatever it took to get her, by any means necessary, he should have been willing to continue to keep her satisfied and happy.

HOW CAN I BE CHARMED?

Clara was captivated by James's smile, good looks, and charismatic personality. I know you are probably thinking it was not possible for him to charm her. Yes, it was. Women who are seeking the protection of a man's affectionate arms fall into many pitfalls and never know how they got there until they open their eyes.

James was also charmed by Clara. She was the one with the power cord. He ran after her while she ran away from him to get him. He was captured by her beauty. She had what most men seek after: long curly hair, light complexion, and a perfect smile. What man wouldn't run behind her?

Women of wisdom, you don't need to be charmed, or to have a charming man make you lose your way. It's time for women to stop settling for anything and wandering away from light, pretending to be seeking Christ. Eve thought she had found the real answer, but it was the answer of death. She lost her spiritual direction after following the voice of the serpent.

**Don't kill the
vision before
the dream appears!**

You know the story of Eve and the serpent and how the serpent beguiled [charmed] her. I am not saying that man is a serpent. However, I am speaking in reference to him being cunning, charming, and convincing.

A man can sometimes convince you to go against what you know is right. Some men may have told you that there's nothing wrong with feeling and touching. That's a lie. It's not true. He will touch and you will die spiritually and emotionally.

It happened with Eve. The enemy saw that Eve was hungry and thirsty for knowledge. In actuality, he set her up for failure. She and her husband were wise and knowledgeable from the beginning. She didn't need the serpent to guide her into anything; they had everything. Everything was created for them to enjoy. They apparently didn't fully understand what they had because they passed their power to the serpent.

Whenever you are uncertain about the power you have, and someone sees the strength that lies within you, they began to pull on you until it is pulled out, and that which belonged to you is deposited into them. The enemy doesn't want you to succeed. The enemy will attempt to kill you before you can birth what's in you.

Approximately twelve years ago, a well-known prophet told me some startling news. She said, "You don't realize how anointed you are. People are taking advantage of your kindness. They are pulling out of you what you don't know you have."

At that time, I didn't know I had anything but love to give. I was anointed to obey God, not man. What I was doing came from the heart. Whatever I had, God gave it to me. His obligation was to cover me and give His angels charge over me, as the Holy Spirit directs me.

You still want to know how you can be charmed by a man. You can be charmed if you are easy, silly, and desperate. In most instances, you are asking, how can I be carried off into the bedroom? This will not be the first bedroom for you, and it will not be the last with that mentality. Sit down somewhere and pray.

A man knows how to ring your bell. There is no hurry to be noticeable. Even now, as you look back at your first meeting with your mate, you are saying in your mind, "I shouldn't have been so easy to give him power over me. I should have made him wait."

In all instances you should have waited, but desperation was present. Desperation gives power into the hands of another person without you ever knowing that it is given until it's too late. A man can sometimes look into your eyes and see that you are hungry and thirsty for attention. He can see that you are empty on the inside, and he will take the opportunity to make good use of you. That's a fact!

The power you and I possess, God gave. Even though you may have little strength, if you have kept God's word and have not denied His name, He will set before you an open door that no man can shut. The enemy will have to come and bow at your feet, and then he will know that God loves you (Revelation 3:8-9).

Be as the blind man who can't see in the natural world. He possesses power which comes from within. His sight comes through touch, and spiritual eyesight comes by hearing the voice of God.

Power is the process in which control is enforced without ever knowing it is given.

Webster's Dictionary defines power as "the ability to do or force; control; authority; influence; right."

Power was given to Adam and Eve. To each of us who are married, He gave power to be fruitful and multiply, power to fill the earth and subdue it. What are we doing to be fruitful? Are souls being saved for His kingdom? Are we speaking to the alcoholic and the prostitute?

We have power to bless. Who are we blessing? After we multiply, fill, and subdue the earth, our greatest reward will be to love our enemies, bless those who curse us, do good to those who hate us, and pray for those who spitefully use us and persecute us (Matthew 5:44-45). Who are you blessing with the power God has given you?

AN OPENED DOOR

Woman of righteousness, if you don't quite understand what you are getting involved with and it is outside the boundaries of integrity, you need to run. Literally run! Please don't look back; you may turn into a pillar of salt. Run, woman of honor, run! Like the women of old would say, "You better run to the city of refuge." Protect yourself. Guard your heart and your body.

God speaks to us, either through someone else or directly, to give instructions for our lives. We should obey and follow them. If we don't, we suffer the consequences of our actions.

It is sad to see a woman embraced by a sweet, charming man with eloquent speech, misrepresenting God's words for a symbol of victory. What is even more devastating is that she can't resist his charisma.

Sadly enough, this is what happens when you forget about God's love and the provision he has made for you. You will walk unprotected through an opened door not designed for you.

You have every opportunity to eat from the trees in the garden, but not from the forbidden tree. By this I mean it is permissible to have dinner, go to a respectable movie, or attend some other cultural event with a single man who is not married, not one who is separated from his wife, waiting for the divorce to finalize.

You must be mindful of the tree that's in the midst of the garden. He may try telling you that it is a good thing to have an intimate relationship (intellectual conversations, kissing, rubbing and touching), and it is not harmful.

Truly, kissing, rubbing, and touching will lead to intimacy. If you are not mature enough to handle that emotion, don't indulge. In God's sight, making love before marriage is unbiblical. If your companion declares differently, that's a lie. God has not changed. Beware of the charmers; there are real perpetrators. For goodness' sake, don't split hairs with them.

HE SEES YOUR VALUE AND YOUR WORTH

Women certainly understand loneliness, and they want that special man to find them. When you are lonely, you are sometimes blinded to the things that are of value. Some men will come with lies and deceptions, convincing you that it is permissible to have sex before marriage. In your heart, you feel this is right. It happens. You felt good. In the recesses of your mind, you are thinking, "It was the best time I've ever had. I never had anybody treat me so tenderly. He listens and he understands. For the first time in my life, I found someone who is trustworthy and dependable."

Wake up, Cinderella! You lost your shoe, not your mind. He sees your value and worth; although you are intelligent, you are also vulnerable. You are an achiever and he treats you as one. Of course he does. You have what he wants: a successful business, a home, car, and two small children. Also, you gave him what he wanted. Now he tells you of his past relationships. How he was abused and misused. All his life he has been seeking a woman just like you. He was tired of being devoured and wounded. He didn't want another woman to bruise his mind, soul, and spirit. But he feels comfort and protection with you. How awesome it was to find you, a good and gentle woman who knows where she is going, who knows how to treat a good man. His desire is to give you his heart. He wants to embrace you with his love. What a wonderful blessing! It is marvelous in his sight that you came into his life.

Sleeping beauty, before making a serious move of transitioning him into your home, open your eyes; you are in a trance. He is making a house appeal. Think about what he is NOT articulating. He may love you because of things you have, and too, you may be an easy prey. You are stubborn and determined to see if he is for real, but weak for intellectual stimulation. He gratified you with words, which caused you to be more concerned about him than your children. A woman in love will kick her children to the curb and move a man in to be the king over them.

Gradually, he comes in changing house rules. He changes what could or can't be seen on television; yet you didn't see yourself change from sleeping on one side of the bed for his comfort. Too, you can't determine when you went from the state of holiness to the state of simple mindedness.

You got a man, but your prayer life changed. You didn't have to seek God anymore; your man became your life and your bright shining light.

You moved too quickly. You got your man, but the husband you prayed for was in close proximity. You remember the day that you and he were in the shopping mall discussing changing the window treatment in your bedroom. Your husband saw you. At that instant, he knew you were his "good thing." But his good thing was walking by with another man.

Before God could answer your prayer for a husband, you chose a man. You perhaps felt that God wasn't going to answer, so you moved ahead of Him. Often, we move ahead of God when we don't feel he sees our value or our worth. He does, and He is before us, working things out for our good. With patience and endurance, the husband you prayed for will come. The faithful, respectful, Bible believing man that you asked God for, that was him who passed you by. The man you wanted to love you and care for your children was passing you by.

You didn't recognize him; he was dirty in his appearance. He just finished a hard day at work. And he didn't look like the man you had pictured, therefore he was on your exempt list.

Remember the prayer you prayed, that he has to be in a professional position with good benefits. That was him. Although you saw him, he was ignored because he wasn't fully clad. But as he passed by, you felt something leaping on the inside of your heart. You didn't understand why, but a message was being transmitted at that time. However, you were too busy exchanging words about window treatments. As he passed by, you should have remembered being on your knees in your prayer room.

You gave up a faithful prayer life for a man who sounds good without a job. In fact, he doesn't have transportation. He has to use your car or SUV, along with your cell phone to seek employment. In the meantime, he does odd jobs, and you have to find a ride home from working long hours. This is not a solid move.

The man you passed by was rejected in haste. His vow to God was never to touch a woman until marriage. He wouldn't have made you break your vow of commitment to God or asked you to give up your car keys and your cell phone. He may have been selfish for your love, but he would not have taken advantage of your honor and body. Without doubt, he'd have understood your dedication to God.

He would have spoken like the other man, telling you of his past relationships and how he was having difficulties understanding why a woman of God, supposedly living a sanctified life, disappointed him as she tried desperately to get him to go against God's law.

He had enough spiritual wisdom not to enter through the door. He respected her and she was angry. That was a silly woman. She left him for refusing to have a conjugal affair.

Prior to meeting your chosen man, he was angry with the other woman; she refused to let him use her without them being married. Then, along came "fine Sally," an open vessel to indulge "ready Freddy."

It's amazing how we sometimes reject our blessings. A rejected man was coming to you in a godly manner without the spirit of deception. But you didn't want him. He may have reminded you of an ex-friend or ex-husband.

Your new found man is opposite of what you like in a man. You are not fitted together. His background is different. He serves a different god, but you are pleased with him. He doesn't believe in holiness or speaking in other tongues.

In Mark 11:24, I read, "What things soever ye desire, when ye pray, believe that ye receive them, and ye shall have them." What happened to the belief system?

He's not willing to change to serve your God, but you are willing to make adjustments to serve his god. You are willing to die on the vine for a fine man.

Rejection isn't new. According to Isaiah, Christ was also rejected. "He was despised and rejected of men; a man of sorrows, and acquainted with grief: and we hid as it were [our] faces from him; he was despised, and we esteemed him not" (Isaiah 53:1).

BLESS THE LORD AT ALL TIMES

Women have been exposed to many things. Therefore, when a well-behaved man does come, they sometime think he must be gay if he doesn't at least attempt to kiss them. This is exactly how God is treated. He is rejected when He is not making things happen in your given time frame.

God sees your value and your worth. Be prayerful, full of purpose, and bless the Lord at all times. If you faint not, your prayers will be answered. Hold on just a little while longer; your Boaz, a man of character, will come; not Bozo, a deceitful silly clown.

In the Book of Ruth, Boaz is identified as a mighty man of wealth (Ruth 2:1). You will also find two significant women, Naomi and

Ruth. Naomi's husband died, and her two sons took wives of women of Moab. One was Orpah and other wife was Ruth. They lived in that land for ten years. Their husbands died, and Naomi, along with her daughters in law, rose that she might leave the country of Moab for Judah. They journeyed with her. On their way to Judah, Naomi said to her daughters, "Go, return to your mother's house. The Lord will be kind to you. And you will find rest."

The daughters wept. But Orpah knew that Naomi was too old to have more sons; if she did have more, by the time they were men, Orpah would have been too old to bear children. She wanted another family. Consequently, she kissed her mother in law and returned to Moab. Ruth, however, remained and said to Naomi, "Entreat me not to leave thee, or to return from following after thee: for whither thou goest, I will go; and where thou lodgest, I will lodge thy people shall be my people, and thy God my God. Where thou diest, will I die, and there will I be buried: the LORD do so to me, and more also, if ought but death part thee and me" (Ruth 1:14-17).

When Naomi saw that Ruth was serious about going with her, they left, heading for Bethlehem. When they reached Bethlehem, old acquaintances were moved to see Naomi. She was saddened in her heart; she went out full [husband and children] and returned empty. She told them not to call her Naomi, but to call her Mara because the Almighty dealt very bitterly with her. Mara means bitter. She thought the Lord did her wrong, or that life was unfair.

You might think that life has been bitter. But if you press on and do not turn back, you will reap the harvest.

She left Bethlehem in search of a better life with her husband and two sons, but she returned with only one daughter in law. Yet downhearted, they arrived at the right time. It was the beginning of barley harvest.

The loving daughter in law Ruth said to her mother in law, "Let me go to the field, and glean ears of corn after him in whose sight I shall find grace" (Ruth 2:2).

Naomi said, "Go, my daughter." She went to the servant who was over the reapers and said to him, "I pray that you let me glean and gather after the reapers among the sheaves" (Ruth 2:3).

Ruth may have been a sorrowful woman, but she wasn't lazy. She went into the field to work, which belonged to Boaz, a close relative of Naomi's deceased husband, to glean ears of corn. She was a stranger in the land, but she was faithful in her duties.

Boaz came into the field, and after seeing Ruth, he made inquiries about her. He said to his servant, "Who is the damsel?" His reply was, "She is the Moabitish damsel who came back with Naomi. She came and been working since early this morning until now, and spent little time in the house" (Ruth 2:5-6).

Boaz may have thought, "She is a relative and a good worker who needs special attention." Examine carefully his remark after he approached her, "Listen my daughter, do not glean in another field, neither leave from here, but abide close to my maidens. I have charged the young men not to touch you. And when you are thirsty, drink from the fountain that the young men have drawn" (Ruth 2:8-9).

Ruth fell on her face to the ground, and in gratitude she spoke, 'Why have I found grace in your eyes, that you should pay attention to me, a stranger?"

Boaz answered her, "I know what you have done for your mother in law since the death of your husband. Also, you left your father and mother came to a land that was unknown, to be her people. God has compensated you for having trust in Him" (Ruth 2:11).

Before Boaz approached her, he had information, history of her faithfulness to her mother in law. Too, the favor of God was upon her, and it is good for a lifetime (Psalm 30:5).

Favor doesn't come because a woman slept with a man. Favor comes from one having faith and confidence in God. To obtain that same favor, do as Ruth: work, be faithful to someone else, and trust God.

CHAPTER 3

Your Hands Make My Spirit Quiver

One shiny day while relaxing in the comfort of my husband's arms, I said to him, "Honey, love me dearly. Take me to a place of excellence, where your sweetness can abide in me, where the touch of your hands makes my spirit quiver, and your smile melts my heart, and your mouth brings forth wisdom. Darling, your love is ever before me. "

Your husband's touch makes your spirit quiver and causes you to do side-straddle-hops. A man's love should be for his wife and his wife only. She is the laughter of his smile, the hope of his tomorrow, and the light that shines in obscurity.

How wonderful it is to be loved by a man with an understanding heart. He sees her strength and sometimes wonders, "How can she fulfill so many tasks?" She rises early in the morning praying for the family, cooking breakfast for her husband before he leaves for work, and getting the children to school.

After that, the dishes are washed, beds are made, and off to work for her. As she arrives to the office, there are messages from staff and co-workers seeking her advice. When does she rest and take time for herself? Only she knows her limitations and can make the decision for personal respite when enough is enough.

Who is this woman? She could be a virtuous woman. But who can find her through so much responsibility? Who can find a virtuous woman? The Bible tells us that a man with an upright heart can find a virtuous woman. He can find her because her price is far above rubies. Her name is great because of her love for God.

As a result, her husband trusts her. She will treat him well. She nurtures, protects, caresses, and loves him. She will enrich his life and will be a helpmeet and not a hindrance all the days of her life (Proverbs 31:10-12). She is clothed with strength and dignity. A virtuous woman is a woman of great wisdom. Kindness is the rule when she gives gentle instructions and advice. Her children call her blessed, and her husband sings praises to her name.

She is diversified. She can move from the kitchen to the bedroom, from being a domesticated housekeeper to a corporate executive, from a devoted wife to a caring mother. You may possibly call her Wonder Woman. No, she's not her.

These things can only be done through her because she's God's woman. She has developed a personal relationship with God, and He has given her strength to do all things that are sufficient for one day.

Without an intimate relationship with God, our intellectual abilities and accomplishments give us the impression that we are making things happen.

Some men and women have climbed the corporate ladder, striving for materialistic solace, and have the strength to maneuver children from one activity to another without being stressful. But this routine can cause one to lose focus on what takes priority.

Sometimes you have to pinch yourself and cross off some appointments to keep the most important priority: worshipping the Father in spirit and in truth. His love is ever before you, and with a sincere heart there is an urgency to be with Him and to love Him with all your heart. Don't miss that quality time by not being in His presence.

Take the time to pray. Plan your day, then ask God if He is pleased with what you have written. If He is not pleased, change after hearing from Him.

Women in ministry, speak with your husbands concerning your daily schedule. When it doesn't meet his agenda, seek God for a change in heart either for you or your husband. Your day and your plan will work perfectly when placed in the holy hands of God. There is not a need to get stressed out over something you can control. I didn't say can't control. I said things you can control.

You can fill in your monthly calendar, but everything on the calendar can't be accomplished in one day. There are seven days in a week, and one of those days is scheduled for rest. Therefore, you have a minimum of four days each month to rest.

God even rested on the seventh day. When are you going to rest? Men and women, your days are not as strenuous as His were. You are not superman or superwoman! But you can do supernatural things through Christ. He gives you the strength to do many things. Even in that, you need to mark on your calendar rest periods for the mind, body, and spirit.

FIRST THINGS FIRST

Close your eyes and think of the times you have been told of your greatness. Think of the small expressions that made you smile. Every woman and man loves to be given a compliment. This may not fit for all, and that select few may choose not to give warm accolades. But women, you should love it when your husbands tell you how great and awesome you are. However, use wisdom; get rest if you want him to whisper gently in your ear all your greatness and awesomeness.

Do not ask too much of the body. Yet, work diligently to achieve various tasks. Don't be slothful, either. You need balance. Learn to be as the virtuous woman who trusts in God.

A woman of wisdom will, at any cost, adorn herself for her husband. Time is never a factor for her to get in position to receive her man.

In the city and in the field you want to be known as an awesome woman, not as a beautiful tired woman who makes provision for God but not for her husband because she failed to find rest.

Hebrews 4:1 tells us to rest. Therefore, in all your doings you must find time to rest and relax. Your husband wants you to spend time with God, and he also wants you to spend quality time with him. He doesn't want you so exhausted that you can't spend intimate time with either.

First things first! Be energized, full of vigor, as excited about spending time with your husband as you are with Christ. After all, your desire is to your husband (Genesis 3:16).

You may worship God, seeing Him as an awesome provider, a friend in need, and a comforter to the lonely. Your husband is, too.

You sometimes see him as provider, friend, and comforter, but you don't always prepare your mind to submit. Adorn your mind, heart, and spirit, and rise up humbly to submit to your husband. Men, give her the same courtesy.

ADVICE FROM THE PAST

We can learn so much from holy women in Biblical days. They knew who they were, and it was easy for them to submit to their husbands without rolling off their lips the famous twenty-first century "why" word. Many women are asking, "Why is it necessary to submit?" Some things are too crucial to ask why, when we can merely do. You don't have to know all the answers.

Those women gave reverence to their husbands as unto the Lord. They demonstrated that a quiet spirit was a great price, which was what Jesus paid. They had good manners in respecting their husbands. They were "not slanderers, not given to too much wine, but teachers of good things. Also, the older women admonished the young women to love their husbands, to love their children, to be good homemakers, discreet, chaste, and obedient to their own husbands, that the word of God may not be blasphemed" (Titus 2:3-5).

Older women were responsible for teaching younger women to have a desire to their husbands, to yearn only for them in wisdom, and to want to satisfy them with all their hearts, souls, and bodies.

Recently, I held a telephone conversation with a middle age woman who wanted to be reunited with her husband. She wanted spiritual advice on what to do.

She said to me, "Financial scrapes and my children separated us. We have been separated for two years, but a short while ago we began conversing about our marriage. I told him that this move was temporary, it was on a trial basis, and he needed to stop doing the things that he was doing for us to stay together. But I will continue to be myself, because I am more knowledgeable than you in the word."

For a moment I couldn't understand what she was saying. I wanted to put my finger down my throat, forcing me to throw up from those ungodly words. But I knew she deserved an answer. I also knew she should have called someone else if she didn't want to know the truth.

I figured that she had not listened to her pastor teaching on how to treat your husband. In my head I thought, *why the separation if she knew more than he did?*

She continued, "I told him that if my children or mother called me, I would leave to go to their rescue." By now, I was feeling really sick on my stomach.

My response was, "Your husband is first. At least, he should be first. You are to desire him and make provision for him, not your mother. I'm not saying that you don't see about your mother and children. But they are not your maximum priority. Honoring him will take dominance. Adult children should be accountable for their actions, and they cannot advise you to go against your husband for them. You must stand up for what is right, love him, and work things out. You asked him to discontinue with what he was doing, and you must dismiss the attitude that you will do what you want. You are wrong for that."

Silence came, and she didn't speak another word. Maybe, just maybe, the separation came from her authoritative mannerism, her explaining how things were going to be in the family. It appeared that she wanted to take over the guidance of the family and to become his head.

My thinking was that while separated she could have studied the word or prayed for wisdom, knowledge, and understanding. Perhaps she should have been like Sarah and really should have given a boost to his ego. Sarah called Abraham lord. You know Abraham was willing to do whatever Sarah asked.

In Genesis chapter 16, he was known as lord, but Sarah didn't mention him as lord until chapter 18. This was a powerful relationship. There were mistakes, but Sarah was willing to support her husband. She was barren, yet she had a handmaid, Hagar, who was young and not barren. Sarah said to her husband, "Because I can't bear children, please go in with my handmaid, and she will conceive a child for me." Abraham listened and went in with Hagar, and she conceived. Her son was called Ishmael.

Abraham was seen as lord to Sarah, and he was willing to satisfy her. Even as Sarah called Abraham lord, the woman who called me should have called her husband lord. Instead, she called him a drunk, and other frustrating names.

Our conversation should have caused her to have a different perspective if she were willing to be modest, respectful, and humble towards her husband. But she wasn't. I believe that with one word of kindness from her lips, she could have changed her husband's life and reunited their marriage. His attitude could have changed rapidly, and then he would have treated her differently according to knowledge. They may have been heirs together for a life of grace. He may have discontinued with the drinking of alcohol and the use of drugs. Sometimes it only takes a smile and a few words to change the heart of a man.

Before hanging up, briefly I asked, "Will you allow him the chance to romance you?" She rejected the idea, and said, "He can't romance me. I can only be intimate and that's it. Right now, he can't do anything else for me. I don't need him touching me and rubbing my body. I only want that one thing. Then, I am satisfied until the next time."

To me, that didn't make sense. She didn't want him to romance her; she wanted him to meet needs and wasn't concerned about working on her marriage from a spiritual perspective.

Whenever someone who is in the place of rebellion receives instructions to do something, he resists, fights back, and kicks against the pricks. As he kicks, he is losing a blessing.

In the book of 1 Peter, the author gives strong yet important information to wives and husbands. To the wives he states, "Be in subjection, subdue, and submit to the obedience of your own husbands."

Strong-willed, strong-minded women continue fighting, not wanting to be humble. In a woman's state of submission or humbleness, I believe, when her husband doesn't understand the Word of God, her obedience through the Word, along with her loving, modest, and pure mannerisms, will change him.

A hint to the wise: a stupid person does stupid things. You don't have to preach to your husband. But be dependent on him. Learn how to adapt to him, and respect him as the head of the family. Don't tell him what the Bible says, live what it states. Then you will get better results. What wisdom to possess!

Instead of trying to prove a point and to have the last word, women can change lives for the kingdom of God by being modest, respectful, honorable, and appreciative. Adore your husband, have a deep sense of admiration for him, and praise him before both family and others. Let him know that you appreciate everything he does. He may not be doing everything right, but you can appreciate him.

Your husband should be your lord in the home, at church, on the job, and everywhere. As you lift up the name of our great God Jehovah, thanking Him for what He has done in your life, woman, thank Him also for your lord, your awesome husband, who found you and chose you as his good thing.

My precious sister, avoid trying to rule and have authority over your husband. Don't be the boss; he is the headship from God. Your conversation of agreement should be with God, not him. Your husband does not need you to be his mother; you are his wife and his lover.

SHE LAUGHED AT THE NEWS

One of the most gratifying attributes of writing your own book is that you can talk about anything. To me, personal communication is subsequent to intimacy in marriages.

Most divorces occur when there is a family financial problem. Without money, women will reject men of conversation and intimacy.

Your finances may not be the best, but if there is sexual communication, your finances will be out of sight for several days. As you take care of the natural obligations, God is in the universe working things out for your financial good.

For if you don't have enough money to pay all your bills, why not enjoy intimacy with your man? The world's system has shown us that sex is not important when there is no money. That system has taught us in the Christian community the dynamics of prostitution. God taught us oneness. Which is more important? When there is not enough money to pay all your bills, go to God and let your request be made known. Then, sow a seed for your harvest. Leave it there and move forth into the arms of your husband.

To have a healthy relationship, intimacy is needed. It consummates marriages. Every time you have sexual intercourse with your husband, you renew your wedding vows. To get to the nitty-gritty, you are only to cease from having sex when you are on your period [menstrual cycle] or fasting with the consent of your husband. As soon as either ends, you are to unite quickly with him so the devil won't get in to plant negative seeds. "Do not deprive one another except with consent for a time that you may give yourselves to fasting and prayer; and come together again so that Satan does not tempt you because of your lack of self-control" (1 Corinthians 7:5).

The twenty-first century woman must be like Sarah, affectionate towards her husband. The Lord spoke to Abraham and told him that his wife would have a son. Sarah was listening from the tent behind him. As she overheard the conversation, she laughed at the news. She didn't laugh because she didn't have feelings for her husband; she laughed because she was past child-bearing years.

Listen, although older women have grown mature, and although young women may not be able to see the breakthrough, neither should give up on God. Though things in your life may tarry, they shall come to pass. Wait on them!

In the meantime, get yourselves together. Couples should be more organized in their finances. Stop shopping and spending every dime you get, trying to impress. Save and budget your money. Seek God for debt management counseling to get organized and back on track.

GROW UP AND STOP DEPENDING ON YOUR PARENTS

Grow up and stop depending on your parents to take care of you. Be reliable for each other and your children. Both of you must take part in this responsibility. A man's desire is to be near his wife and children. But if you let grandparents keep them all the time, you will lose respect.

Tell your parents that it's good that they want to help out, but you need your children back. Grandparents will spoil your children and teach them new rules. Take back control of your children; a tremendous change will be seen in your husband.

Grandparents may be somewhat upset with this thought, but it's the truth. They ought to release their grandchildren to grow up with their own parents, and grandparents need to build closeness with each other.

You may be laughing at this, but you are laughing to keep from facing the truth. Parents ought to take care of their own children. Grandparents, if married and still together, should build intimacy together instead of hiding behind the grandchildren.

Fire is still in the coals. They are gray, ready to cook. If you need to see the flames, poke them. They want to be rekindled. As fire is rekindled, you are not too elderly to regenerate old feelings. Let the grandchildren stay home. This is a good time for talking and getting it right.

Candlelight dinners or a stroll in the neighborhood are good. Pull out the bicycles and ride together. For the bedroom, he may need Viagra. You may need to tone down the noise and not rush him to get up. Lie still and relax. Grandparents, let the children stay home! Stop laughing! This message is essential to your success in life. Take a walk by the river and enjoy the scenery as you embrace and hold hands. Watch a love story and get your groove on. Running away from the real issue will never solve your hidden situation. Whatever you do, be real and let the fire burn hidden thoughts.

CHAPTER 4

Talk to Him, He'll Listen

Commit thy works unto the Lord, and thy thoughts shall be established. The Lord hath made all things for himself: yea, even the wicked for the day of evil. Every one that is proud in heart is an abomination to the LORD: though hand join in hand, he shall not be unpunished. By mercy and truth iniquity is purged: and by the fear of the LORD men depart from evil. When a man's ways please the LORD, he maketh even his enemies to be at peace with him.

Proverbs 16:3-7

*O*nce married, commit your body to your husband or to your wife. From the point of saying, "I do," you lose control over your body. He or she has control! Isn't it amazing that every time you bathe, you are washing his or her body with much compassion and tenderness?

**A sound heart is
the life of the flesh.**

A close friend once told me that her husband was the greatest, and made terrific love as he stimulated her mind. Two words, *love* and *stimulation,* caught my attention. Beyond that, I didn't need to know about her love life. To me, they had a beautiful marriage, one that I thought epitomized what marriage was all about. Her husband humbly bowed at her feet. She was an exceptional housekeeper and mother. From the outside looking in, they were extraordinary. They held hands, complimented each other, and attended church together. They were an encouragement to other married couples. Single men and women perceived them as having the perfect marriage. I wanted a marriage just like theirs. I needed that tenderness in a man to call husband. He worked and brought his paycheck home. They sorted out bills and paid them together. She took care of the home inside, and he managed the outside landscape.

One day, this loving woman opened up to me in confidence about her marriage. I thought, *What could be wrong with their marriage?*

She began by saying, "In the real world, my relationship is different. It is not what other people think."

What is she talking about? I thought to myself.

My heart was broken when she told me that her husband's outer appearance was different from his home appearance. He had two faces, one for the public and one in the home. In the home, he didn't live a respectful life in front of her and their son. Her husband treated her as the weaker vessel by handling her rough like sandpaper. He used profanity and was judgmental. He also had frequent boxing matches with his wife. She was small in size; she couldn't handle the knocks and bruises. She paused and said, "In his anger, he is not fighting me; he sees someone else."

I said, "That might be true, but you are receiving those hard blows."

She was the tenderness of her husband, the tears that he couldn't seem to cry; she was the softness of the relationship when it was difficult for him to succumb emotionally. She further stated that his anger stemmed from his childhood. His father left the family, and he thought he contributed to that loss. His mother was his protector. She told him from the time he was a small child that a woman should never control a man and that a woman should never give a man advice.

Every time my friend recommended an idealistic goal to reach, either family or personal, her husband felt that she was usurping authority and that she thought she was better than he. He couldn't handle it, therefore he fought her.

My God, what a waste of a man to call husband! Women, keep the faith, and don't give up. Don't let this turn you off. God hears your prayers for transformation, and He sees your tears.

Sad to say, my friend and her husband separated. That happy marriage, which I wanted to imitate, was sour and stinking. Quickly, my desire for this type of marriage was rescinded. I learned early that they were a perfect match for each other. He was meant for her and not for me. I would not have tolerated the hits and blows. From then on, my heart was set on God sending me a man like Himself.

One ingredient was missing from my friend's marriage. She and her husband forgot the wedding vows to honor, obey, provide, love, and respect in sickness and in health. She didn't see him as being her lord, and he forgot, during the course of the relationship, that she was his queen, or his good thing.

OPEN YOUR MOUTH AND SPEAK

As never before, it's time that wives communicate effectively with their husbands on all points, in complete honesty. This is your season to speak the truth. The truths penetrated in your hearts must prevail. Truth will make a woman free when she speaks it. Therefore, wives, open your mouths and speak the truth in love.

There is a need for truth. Even if your husband gets irritated, the truth is inescapable. Look for an opportune time to be open. Usually, we are dishonest with our mates because either we don't want our feelings hurt or we don't want to hurt their feelings. We need to stop playing games and just tell the truth. We have been together long enough that we can be truthful with one another.

The truth will turn you every which way but loose. And, it will also break you into small pieces. Afterward, you shall come forth as pure gold.

Recently, I told my husband that he doesn't do what I ask. He replied, "That's not true. I do what you ask me to do most of the time. I hear you; and eventually I'll do it. I just don't move when you want me to move."

The truth was spoken from his lips, and those words gave me something to consider. For a moment I thought, *He wasn't wrong.* He doesn't move when I expect, and he does do what I ask, for the most part, at his own pace.

Sometimes, I don't think I'm framing my words correctly to get him to move as effectively for me as he does for others. I don't want to have power over him. Yet in the midst of an operation, I require help, and I want the help to come then, not later. Later might be too late. My motto is, why put off for later what you are equipped to do now? We are not to be slothful in business [our dealings].

How often do wives say to their husbands, "I want you to have a seat. It is essential that we talk, but I don't want you to brush me off?" For the most part, as we articulate, we don't want our words to give the wrong impression or to be taken lightly. Are we walking on eggshells? Our words are precious and spoken in love. Though often silent, sometimes you have to open your mouth to speak of things that are overwhelming you.

Tell him, "Honey, thank you for allowing me the privilege to come into your presence to speak from my heart. As you listen and internalize what I say, I ask that you not interrupt me. Even if you think the conversation is complete, please don't interrupt me. There are six ideas that I believe can improve our relationship. Baby, I request that you:"

1. *Take a vacation.* Let's do weekend trips, so we can be alone: no children, no grandchildren, no pets, but only us being lovers. Let's just take time for us, where we can be intimate.
2. *Enjoy our night.* The night which we set aside for us, let's do special things: a movie is neat; a stroll on the beach is an

ideal medicine; or holding hands near a warm fire lights up our lives.

3. ***Study the Bible with me.*** It will propel me to mediate more on the word. Holding hands while praying will be an extra enchantment. I just want to be near you to behold your strength, power, and energy.

4. ***Articulate what you need from me to improve our relationship.*** I am not selfish, except to indulge you. I am willing to do whatever is within the will of God to satisfy your needs and delight your wants. However, I will not violate a law for you. For clarification, I won't steal, lie, deceive others, defraud a neighbor, or rob him for you. Neither will I make people eat bitter food and drink poisoned water for your glory: commit adultery and live with that lie while strengthening the hands of evildoers (Jeremiah 23:15). Honey, I love you, and I know that "love covers a multitude of sins" (1 Peter 4:8). Some time back, before I met the Lord, you could have gotten me maybe to think about transgressing a law. But I will not now. I am a holy woman, full of the spirit, living a life of righteousness. I'm not equipped to violate God's law.

5. ***Be an example for the children.*** Teach them to clean up what they mess up. Be that good example by putting up the shaving cream, hanging up your clothes, and replacing your shoes in the shoeboxes in the closet. They shouldn't be stored all over the house. Thank you for putting the tools in the toolbox and for sorting through the box near the computer. Keep what is important, and allow me to throw away what hasn't been used. You squeeze the toothpaste from the bottom, but it is annoying to see the children squeezing it from the top and leaving it open, with toothpaste on the counter and floor. Help our children to do better.

6. ***Treat me as the apple of your eye.*** Wine and dine me as your precious queen. Take me shopping. Have a desire to hug me in the mall and hold my hand.

Esteemed husbands do not think these are simple things, and it is strange that we are speaking this. These small things are important to us. We are whom you chose. We are a gift from God: loving, gentle, meek, and humble. Adore us, respect us, charm us, and appreciate us highly above others; we are your good thing. And we want to improve communication and our relationship.

SOME MEN MAY REJECT THIS!

Listen, husbands, this is good talk. Encourage your wife and make a positive point that you are going to improve. Help with the children, prepare a meal, or take them out during the week.

There are some men who may reject this suggestion by saying, "I married her to do for me, the children, and the house. I'm working, and that's all I can do. I'm tired. I work long hard hours. All she does is stay home; she has an easy life."

Nonsense! You know you can be challenging. When you get out of your clothes, you leave them in the middle of the room. You comb your hair and leave hair in the comb, over the sink, and on the floor. Every thirty minutes, you are calling to check up on her. And what's worse, some mornings after leaving for work, you double back with a phone call or a visit to the house. For what purpose are you doing this? Why are you trying to break her sleep pattern or prayer time? You chose that she not work. If you have changed your mind, talk to her.

On the other hand, a man who is sensitive to his wife's needs and wants to be an improved husband shouldn't be like other men who are bossy and want to dominate women. These ideas are a few good nuggets for the man who wants a good life.

- *Never be bossy; never ever dominate her.* God gave you power, control, dominion and authority over things, not your wife. You are not to treat her as anything defiled or anything less than a child of God. Take time to listen to her. Avoid making decisions for her before talking with her. You are the king, not the tyrant.
- *Things will work out when you and your wife come together.* Communicate, pray, and fast for what you want. Know without

doubt that you are called to inherit a blessing from God, and your children will also have that inheritance.

- *Both of you should be of one accord.* Be of the same mind, love each other, and be tenderhearted and humble.
- *You can stop with the late night email courtship.* It's not real, but your wife is. The emails are only an illusion of grandeur. The real touch is with her. Don't try to insult her when she asks you about the courtship. She is trying to save you from being hurt and attempting to save her marriage. You may say, "It's her imagination." Then you should have no problem introducing her to your new computer friend. They need to get to know each other. Tell your cyberspace friend that she is your darling wife and the mother of your two beautiful children. Allow them the opportunity to become chat room bosom buddies, if it's all innocent. You may have gotten caught, but pray for personal closeness. Offer up to God a prayer of protection and guidance with deep affection and devotion for the person you love. Never render evil for evil, but do unto her as you would have her do unto you.
- *Don't stand for anyone to criticize your wife.* Though you are experiencing unhappiness in your relationship, you must defend her! Inform your family that because she is your wife, you refuse to allow them to treat her disrespectfully.
- *"Husbands, love your wives, just as Christ also loved the church* and gave Himself for her, that He might sanctify and cleanse her with the washing of water by the word, that He might present her to Himself a glorious church, not having spot or wrinkle or any such thing, but that she should be holy and without blemish. Consequently husbands ought to love their own wives as their own bodies; he who loves his wife loves himself. For no one ever hated his own flesh, but nourishes and cherishes it, just as the Lord does the church" (Ephesians 5:25-29).
- *Men, you must know that you and your woman are joint-heirs of the grace of God.* Grace is seen as the God kind of love demonstrated from your heart to another. It is the favor that cannot be repaid. It is also the beauty that shines from

within to the outward appearance where man can see the virtue of a woman, and she can feel the joy that radiates from him. In the state of togetherness, you can know and feel the presence of God demonstrated through His grace called love.

- ***Women, there is nothing wrong with you telling your husband what you enjoy.*** Is it the movement of the bath glove? Do you love how he strokes your body? Tell him that it thrills your mind and soul and you want more of those type demonstrations at least three times a week. He will be together with your thoughts.

- ***Tell your husband that you will always love and respect him.*** When it's impossible to be intimate because of health reasons, let him know that you are creative in that area, and you, without his worry, know how to caress and embrace his body and mind. You know when to turn off the light.

CHAPTER 5

Talk to Her;
She'll Understand

But speaking the truth in love, may grow up into
him in all things, which is the head, even Christ.
Ephesians 4:15

*I*f only he knew that expressed feelings from his lips would reach her heart, he would speak continuously words that would move her to do whatever he speaks. Too often, there are many complications that prevent us from relating softly with each other. Proverbs 15:1 tells us that "A soft answer turns away wrath."

So often women don't know when they are blessed and highly favored by their husbands, especially when they desire to talk. Quietness with meekness should call us to close our mouths, keep our ears open, and close our eyes that we may see spiritually and hear with a smooth understanding what they desire from us.

Many men don't talk with their wives, for if a husband tells a wife something and she disapproves, then she's screaming, yelling, cussing, and fussing. She goes to the extreme in throwing her weight around to gain power and control, and he withdraws, never to mention anything to her again. The door to communication is shut tight.

Likewise, some men don't tell their wives anything of importance because they don't want the complaining. The wife constantly nags, pulling her husband off to the side, complaining or raising havoc softly in public when he doesn't fully understand her language. Isn't it annoying to see a woman pull a man to the side to scold him in public? It is somewhat embarrassing to see a man in the corner with his wife whispering to him as if he were in time-out for disobeying his fifth grade teacher. For that reason, a woman usually can't get her husband to do anything productive.

From a man's perspective, when he brings his wife into his environment and opens up to her, he doesn't want his wife frustrated about money, poor health, children, or employment. Most men desire for their wives to stay home and care for the children. But let's be realistic. The majority of men don't make enough money to solely provide properly without a woman's income.

There are various reasons to consider why he can't make it without her paycheck. He could be a poor manager of money, or not make enough money due to lack of education, illness, retirement, or other reasons. He needs her help. In spite of that, he wants to have a warm conversation with her. He wants feelings to die. Feelings are the root of most of the confusion in the home and in the workplace. Lies are derived from feelings.

Today we are fine, and tomorrow we don't remember talking about our feelings or emotions because we are confused whether we love or hate. Feelings tell us that we love without compromise, and the next hour we are explaining why we love conditionally.

Feelings are like memory loss. My mother has slight dementia. Some days she is great, and other days she can be overwhelming. On those days, she is extremely active. As she calms down, I'll speak with her about her behavior, and she'll say, "Oh baby, I didn't do that. I don't remember, but it won't happen again." What won't happen again? She doesn't remember. Feelings that I maintain concerning her actions will be crazy. She doesn't remember. Feelings can be lost and forgotten for a successful relationship.

KEEP YOUR FOOT OUT OF YOUR MOUTH

Your husband understands that you have a unique relationship with God. He knows that you are diligent in your faith in the congregation of people, yet your feelings change with him at home. You are slack in your prayer life and reading the Word. But you are stating to the public, "Although he is the head, I am not blessed because of him. He's living a lie. He failed or disappointed me."

Keep your foot out of your mouth, and praise that man. You will be blessed with his presence in church. He will bless you above measure if you keep quiet. That's what you have been praying for: blessings and his attending church. Please be quiet, and settle down. Then if you release your feelings and praise him, they will materialize. Don't get offended and be on lockdown for days, weeks, or months. Praise your man, and see the glory of the Lord work in his life.

Another problem is that you have wanted him to come to bed with you, but he waits until you are asleep to come to bed. Change your thought pattern, and see him desiring to sleep with you. Walk before him in a sexy gown. He feeds into that behavior. It doesn't have to fit, but it must come off easily.

Your nagging is your husband's excuse for not becoming spiritually wealthy. Normally, you are busy being the spiritual head because you don't think he reads the Word. Change your mindset, and see the glory of God move on him. Also, become a true worshipper. God will change things for your husband as you praise and worship Him.

The truth is that you can study the Word together. At this time, the words that fall from your lips discourage your husband from sharing anything. Also, instead of encouraging him, you always threaten him. Leave the man alone.

The Bible states that if he doesn't study or know the Word, he may be won by your mannerisms when he observes your chaste conduct accompanied by fear (1 Peter 3:1-2). He needs to see that attitude in you. Humble yourself before your husband. Fall at his feet (1 Samuel 25:24).

SATISFACTION GUARANTEED

Can I talk to you, my sister who can identify with purpose? Okay, I'll talk to the modern woman who will understand where we're going with this. There comes a time when a man needs to put a silly woman in her place. Don't you agree? Well, possibly not!

Your husband doesn't just watch sports, he listens to the Trinity Broadcasting Network (TBN), and The Word Network. He knows what the Word is saying about his life. He knows his position as the head. The reason it seems as if he is out of place is that he is trying to bring stability into the home. You keep moving, running away from him, and he is trying to find you. There are some things that he wants you to know.

- *You are to be his crown, not his clown.* Stop calling him silly and stupid. Don't give the impression that you are more versed in the Word than he. If you feel that way, use wisdom. The Bible says, "It is better to dwell in a corner of the housetop, than with a brawling woman in a wide house" (Proverbs 21:9). At the corner of the housetop, you can see and experience the various seasons better than when in companionship with a brawling wife.
- *He is tired of sleeping in the guestroom or the doghouse.* Your negative speech places your husband in these rooms until you are sound asleep before he gets into bed. Then, he wakes an hour early to avoid your chattering. He states from the depths of his heart that he wants you to cease the nagging and pray in the Holy Ghost. He wants to see and hear you praising and magnifying God.
- *He will attend church with you* when you began treating the home as your sanctuary, a holy place.
- *He wants to make passionate love.* Sexual gratification shouldn't be hard for you, but it is. Yet you want him to prove his love by giving you material things. In essence, you may be pushing him away with strong, harsh words. He doesn't want you to reject his affections. He is tired of being told that you are always sick with a cold or that one of the children does not

66

feel well. He understands and appreciates what you do, but he wants you to consider his needs also. He wants you to satisfy his needs, and he wants to give you what you want. Work with him by not sleeping in your clothes.

To some women, intimacy is a very difficult subject to cover. Sexual conversations can be uneasy if there is no intimacy in the family. Sex originated with God. Sexual intercourse was God's first command. He told Adam and Eve to "Be fruitful, and multiply, and replenish the earth" (Genesis 1:28)

Your continued attachment to past relationships may make it impossible for you to transfer your affections to your husband. Every chance you get, you contemplate how Robert gave you money, Ford Sr. took you shopping, Danny paid the down payment on your car, and Johnny caressed your body. Let it die. They don't remember you or the feeling. You are a thing of the past. The thrill and the feeling are gone. Let it die. Your past is over! See your present; then move to the future.

I was at a friend's house one evening when her phone rang. It was her sister. I could hear happiness in my friend's voice, but suddenly tears ran down her cheek. Her voice changed, and her male companion drew closer to hold her hand as she continued to talk. By then I was ready to go home. I stood up and waved goodbye, but she beckoned for me to sit. I sat down, and soon after she got off the telephone. She was crying because her sister told her, "The man you are with is my old boyfriend, and you have no reason to be dating him. In fact, he is too old for you. And I am angry with you for going behind me."

When she completed speaking those words, her boyfriend said, "Why is she angry? That was so long ago. You were not born; and, too, I don't remember the feeling."

Release the feeling and let it die. Your man is hurting, and you can stop the hurt. Reflect back on the day you met. You were vibrant and alive. You held his hands; now you don't. You laundered his clothes; now you can't because you are tired. He has to spray Febreze on his clothes to kill the odor. Girlfriend, you are wrong for that. Febreze doesn't work on everything.

Here is some additional information to improve a loving marriage.

1. *He wants the two of you to sit down and develop a plan of events for the home.* It's going to take time and discipline, but he knows it will work.

2. *He wants you to pick up behind the children.* Put dirty clothes in the hamper. Put trash in the garbage, not all over the house. Train the children how to clean the house, brush their teeth, and comb their hair.

3. *He knows you have a third checking account and a money market saving with your mother.* That's wrong, sister. He doesn't understand why he wasn't asked about this. He thinks you are hiding something. You two are one flesh. Where did the third party come from? If you needed another person's name on the account, why didn't you ask his mother? As my goddaughter said to me once, "My bad, I forgot!"

4. *You know he doesn't want you wearing hair rollers to bed.* He prefers a silk scarf draped about your head to maintain your hairdo. Submit to his simple request.

5. *A big, sloppy t-shirt is not going to turn him on sexually.* He prefers you wearing the black, red, or white negligee. Trash the pajamas with holes. Talk it over with her until she gets it in her conscience.

6. *He wants you to know that he is making preparation to lose weight.* He is on a special nutritional plan. The fifty pounds are coming off. He is backing away from the table, drinking water, and walking. You don't have to be ashamed anymore. You can be seen with him. It would be a blessing if you walked with him.

7. *Don't preach to him, but live a good life before him.* It's inappropriate to either position your finger in his face or wring your neck like a slut on the streets who stands wide legged looking for a man. **Don't Be Slanderous Towards Your Husband.**

8. *Depend on him.* Learn how to adapt to him, and regard him as the head of the family. You are not to be rude, sarcastic, and discourteous when he is inappropriate or out of the will of

God. Don't merely tell him what the Bible states. Live what it states, and you will get better results. Furthermore, never put him down; always build him up. Don't be slanderous towards your husband in the midst of his friends by dashing your eyes in disbelief as he speaks. You know you're wrong for that. Don't try to boost your character and gash his heart. That's not a well-behaved representation of a happy marriage.

9. *What goes on sexually with you and your husband is your business and your business only.* It should not be discussed with anyone except him. For goodness sake, don't tell your mother or your girlfriend that your man doesn't satisfy you. That is called insulting. You are communicating this to the wrong person. Tell him what he can do to improve your sex life. What wisdom it is to be assertive, to welcome him home with a pleasant smile, or to tell him how great his lovemaking is. Sometimes, you have to call things into existence if you are unable to communicate. Then, too, demonstrate what you want! Remember this, it is very important.

WISDOM IS THE BEGINNING OF KNOWLEDGE

Every married couple has disagreements. Yet there is more than one way to solve problems. Instead of trying to prove a point and have the last word, you can change lives for the kingdom of God by being modest, respectful, honorable, and appreciative.

Adore him. Have a deep sense of admiration for him, and praise him before the family and others. Let him know that you appreciate everything he does.

Listen, you'll get what you want, and he's happy. Women, if you don't have wisdom, get it. Wisdom is the beginning of knowledge. A woman of wisdom or a wise woman wins souls! A husband who is not saved can be your first soul won.

As you communicate to him in a respectful manner, you honor, appreciate, and hold him in high esteem. Enjoy your husband, and put no one else ahead of him.

CHANGE THE ATMOSPHERE WITH PLEASANTNESS

In 2001 a conversation began with a family member who was angry concerning some things that his wife was doing. He expressed his frustration to me, and I want to share it with you. Women, please avoid complimenting another man without complimenting your husband in the same manner. Never tell another man of his greatness and dispel that information from your man. It is not a good thing to discuss your sex life with another person, except with your pastor or a medical professional. Listen carefully when your husband is talking. By no means accuse him of another woman. Change the atmosphere with pleasantness.

A submissive wife will on no account allow her affection to be as an outward appearance. Her appearance should not be as the outward adorning with make-up and plaiting of the hair (1 Peter 3:3), her success, her education, her money, her personal enriched status in life, but as the inward adorning and beauty of the hidden person of the heart with great charm that will not fade for her husband.

Women, as the weaker vessel, should be treated lovingly and with respect. Women, on the other hand, should be in subjection to their husbands, yielding to their power and authority with a soft approach.

Yielding to a husband does not mean that a woman can't voice her opinion. Wisdom is the beginning of knowledge! Search inwardly, seeing if you are submissive or merely trying to disguise. Outwardly, you may have it going on, but inwardly, you perhaps argue with his decision making ideas. You may think in your mind, "What is he doing to me?" Negative aggression may be on your mind to change whatever he thought, to actually do things your way.

It is all right to surrender yourself without hesitation to your husband. Honestly it is. For the breakthrough of blessings to flow in your life, you have to give up those past challenges that almost destroyed your marriage.

WITH A REMORSEFUL HEART

My brother, your wife needs to hear this from you. Talk to her, she'll understand. Men who are not in a relationship with God usually can't accept suggestions or recommendations well from the opposite sex. However, this is the time to ask men to talk to their mates. Women are willing and waiting to hear you say something of this nature,

"Darling, I realize that I have not always treated you with respect. I did not listen attentively to you when I wanted to watch sports. But you didn't appear angry, and you found other means to entertain yourself as I watched television. I come to you with a remorseful heart, asking forgiveness for neglecting you. Life is filled with many things that preoccupy our minds. Time is crucial for us. And I'm speaking to set our house in order. Our marriage has not been filled with roses and chocolate-coated strawberries. Forgive me for sitting back, waiting on you to take the first step. From the depth of my heart, I want us to have a worthwhile conversation. I enjoy running your bath water, filling the tub with scented raspberry bubbles, sea clay soaking solution, and therapeutic bath salt soak to extract tiredness from your revered body. I love drying off your body and massaging it with various fragrance oils. You are the sunshine of my life.

Out of the bedroom, I need for you to allow me to do more for you. It gives me satisfaction to open and close the car door, holding your hand as you graciously slide both legs out of the car with that gigantic, pretty smile you have. Don't ever stop me from grasping your hand as we walk through the mall. It gives me great pleasure to be your husband. Thank you for accepting to be my wife. You are important to me.

Of course, we have had disappointments and we have been disagreeable. But, we are different individuals. We will perhaps disagree on numerous things until we die, but can we agree to disagree even in truth.

I can be cantankerous, moody, hateful, and depressed without reason. That's not what I choose to do. I've seen this behavior in men who didn't take advice easily from anyone. They try to work with others, to fit comfortably into the work force, but they reject every idea with a strong comment on why it doesn't work. I also notice them at lunch. I see how they engage in controversial conversations, making mountains out of molehills for no apparent reason.

You knew something was wrong with me. But you didn't understand why the disagreeable behavior. I know how much you'd pray for me, asking God to move me into a position to see your submission. I sense in my soul that God is about to answer your unwavering prayers. Never give up on me.

Honey, I also need help with my diet Coke consumption. I need this for my health. Really and truly, it is sixty pounds I want to lose. My body has changed, along with my attitude. When I was smaller, my ideas were better and more creative. Now, I am tired and fatigued for the most part. I don't want to go anywhere. I am constantly in pain with migraine headaches. Diabetes has me drained and exhausted. I have weak knees, and I am always depressed. Prozac is my medication. No wonder things are as they are. But I want more from our relationship. I need you to be close to me. I am weak, and I appear to fall as I reach for your hands to hold me steady; I seriously could do with your love and support."

HE PULLS YOU CLOSER TO HIM

In all my years of being married to Herb, I feel closer to him when he gets closer to the Lord. Somehow, as I move closer to him, I become an integral part of his life, spirit, soul, and body. He is sensitive to my needs and has patience to listen to my thoughts.

The closer your husband gets to God, the closer he pulls you to himself. And he will then listen to your suggestions and sometimes your complaints. Furthermore, listening doesn't move him out of a leadership position, but brings you close to his side.

You'll become a team because he is giving the weaker vessel an opportunity to express her true feelings without putting her down or slamming doors in her face.

After all, she is his helper. He is not giving up control.
They are operating in the authority given by God.

We know that there is a time and season to all things. The only time for a man to express his feelings in a loving manner and still get his point across to his mate is now.

BY ANY MEANS NECESSARY

Remember, husband, you articulated to get your wife. You can surely communicate effectively to keep her. She doesn't need a whimpering man who thinks that if he says anything he will be on trial. What does a trial have to do with anything?

By any means necessary, talk with accuracy and good sense. A stern, negative speaking man is not wanted. Only an even-tempered, positive man who knows the benefit of communicating properly is desired in these times.

Therefore, men, you can suspend raising your voices and screaming, "I'm the man! I'm the head of this family." If you comprehend this truth, then be the man of God. You don't have to demonstrate it by lifting up your pants leg with a strong attitude of pride. This is a new day, and we are educated to that expression. We know that whenever a man speaks in that tone, his wife rules the household, the finances, the sex life, and every area of the family. Be careful of what you say out loud.

I'm sorry! I didn't mean to go there. But please relax in your spirit. I do not mean to embarrass anyone, simply to help. At times it can be complicated talking to a bull-headed woman. That kind is not teachable. An unreachable woman who cannot be taught is given over to much fasting and prayer. Men have to pray to God for wisdom and get understanding before talking to her.

She may be forceful, but she has some good qualities. She takes care of your house. She cooks, cleans, and manages things. Every morning, you give her an assignment, and she completes the task. She reminds you to take your vitamins and hypertension medications. But a conversation with her can be erratic.

Prepare yourself emotionally and spiritually before talking gently to your wife. She'll comprehend that you don't want her fussing in public setting: in a restaurant with the waitress, with a sales representative, or with a department store manager. Let her know that you don't appreciate her pushing you out of the way to take over a conversation when she should have been praying for peace and favor.

At home, have a skillful dialogue with her. Let her know that she can't invite visitors over for dinner without your approval. That's a pet peeve with you.

My brother, please unravel. Discard from your thoughts that raising your voice and being rough can only help your wife. That is not the way to win her heart. Talk to her; she's capable of listening. She is not dumb, stupid, or crazy. Remember that you found her, and if you feel that way, then you must be the first partaker of that behavior. Ask yourself if you clearly communicated how you wanted your wife to behave in public and in the home?

The Bible says to teach her in the way she should journey. "Let a woman learn in silence with all submission" (1 Timothy 2:11). "The aged women likewise, that they be in behaviour as becometh holiness, not false accusers, not given to much wine, teachers of good things" (Titus 2:3).

At my husband's retirement in 1998, I wrote him a poem. He was surprised when his supervisor asked me to speak. He didn't know what I was going to say. The poem brought tears to his eyes. From that moment, he began to change. These are words I wrote to him:

Love is the fragrance of incense and myrrh. It is the sunshine that illuminates from the rain with a bright rainbow of your thoughtfulness. Love is the embrace of your smile, expressing how you tenderly caress my heart with satisfaction, reassuring me that all is well in my soul and spirit. Love is the teardrops of laughter when you tickle my body; love is recycling the peace, joy, and happiness of your words that delivers me from stress and anxiety. Love becomes intimate when you hold me in your arms and speak to me from your heart and mind with wisdom from God. Thank you, darling, for your intimate love!

Every time I see those words, it touches my heart to know that we can tell the truth even when we are angry, upset, or mad. We can think on the touch, the smile, and the way he or she walks. The way she does her hands or the cute way he holds his head brings cheerful thoughts.

Holy woman of God, your smile, personality, and the way you treat him can win an unbelieving husband. Godly wife, be in subjection to your own husband and win his heart. If he is not a Christian, and if he doesn't obey the word of God or the preached gospel, he can be won by your conversation.

Esther demonstrated to us how a husband could be won. As she prayed for her particular situation, she fasted before entering the king's presence. Her conversation was coupled with respect, love, and adoration.

A wife who is saved should have a biblical understanding of the Word and live what she knows before trying to get her husband into that place of acceptance. She is his marriage partner, not his minister. Although marriage is ministry, and she may sound like God, she does not serve as his minister. Instead of preaching, she should clothe herself in righteousness and peace.

Marriage came into existence after God created Adam. He declared, "It is not good that man should live alone" (Genesis 2:18).

On seeing the woman, Adam said decidedly, "This is now bone of my bones and flesh of my flesh; she shall be called Woman, because she was taken out of Man" (Genesis 2:23). This passage also emphasizes the truth that "a man shall leave his father and mother and be joined to his wife, and they shall become one flesh" (Genesis 2:24). Her responsibility is to honor her husband (Ephesians 5:22).

Part Two

"I'm Single; Is There a Word for Me?"

Train up a child in the way he should go: and when he is old, he will not depart from it.

Proverbs 22:6 KJV

No one seems to understand that I have hurts and pains; I am attracted to the opposite sex, but I don't understand these feelings. Can someone help me to channel my feelings and emotions? I desire to do the right thing, but I don't know what is right when I can't compare it to wrong. Help the children; help us teenagers. We are drowning in our own self-indulgence.

Love us to health; create a healthy environment that we may prosper in all things. Be patient and help the young people to understand life.

Chapter 6

Teenagers, Coping With Development

"They don't understand me. I want to be left alone. I just want to have a friend. I am tired of the abuse," Ra'quel said in a recent interview. Like most teenagers, she felt that her parents didn't particularly care for her, and they were her enemies.

At the tender age of fifteen, Ra'quel was pregnant. Both parents were shocked and stunned to hear of her pregnancy. But her mother took it the hardest. She wanted her perfect little girl to graduate from high school and to attend college without any blemishes on her record. Now, her mother thought, she had blown it.

Technically speaking, there is a blemish on Ra'quel's record. For the rest of her life, she has the privilege of raising her son. Her education is only on hold temporarily, until the doctor releases her to attend school again.

In most cases of a pregnancy, we feel that a girl's or a boy's life is over. It's not over, but there is a temporary delay. What happened in Ra'quel's case is that she didn't feel love growing up. Her biological father died while she was in her mother's womb. However, she has a fantastic stepfather, who treats her as his own. Somehow, she felt disconnected from her family and felt nobody loved her. She began to look for love in others who would accommodate her needs. She met and fell in love with Nathan, who was known as a lover and roughneck. He told her that he loved her and that the only way to provide evidence of her love was to be intimate in her affection. The type of affection they had ended in pregnancy.

Like most teenagers, her affections turned from love to hate. She hated Nathan during and after the pregnancy. She refused to communicate with him. In her mind, she wanted a baby. And she would treat him or her with so much love that he or she will grow up to love her dearly.

For the most part, teenagers really want a friend to tell all their problems. In this case, as in others, the baby becomes the mother's best friend. Both roles can't be performed when you become a parent. A parent must train, teach, reproach, nurture, reprove, love, and change diapers. A best friend is someone with whom you don't want to have discord. You want a friend to be by your side and agree with everything you say or do. A parent has to make choices, and letting a child have his or her way is not the solution.

Even though we are living in a different dispensation, all of us want to be loved. Young adults and teenagers want to know that there is someone for them. As a child, most parents have experienced some of the same feelings as you teenagers are encountering today.

Teenagers may want to be loved in a different way. Their desire is to have someone with whom they can hang out, play games, share common interests, and chill. They also want popularity to lessen loneliness.

Teenagers, coping with development can be overwhelming. Some feel they are old and mature enough to date. I wasn't permitted to date until I was seventeen, and even then, I still wasn't prepared for dating. I heard things from friends who dated before me, but I didn't understand the concept. Teenagers want to hold hands, kiss a little, and talk on the telephone every day until the midnight hours. That sounds wonderful! But things must be done in moderation. Too, what about school work and chores around the house?

My personal observation is that teenagers shouldn't talk on the telephone daily to any one boy or girl. A time during the week should be scheduled for them to talk, and not for more than fifteen minutes.

Talking leads to an action plan; then that plan can work its way into the bedroom, the back seat of a car, a late park experience, a beach scene, or a side of any building performing sexual acts. You are probably saying, "This is not me. This will never happen to me. I am not that type of person."

Some parents are thinking, *No. This does not describe my child. They were educated and raised better than to get sexually involved before marriage.* It might be true, but things do happen.

This message is not an attack; it is only to assist parents to see how they can reinforce moral and biblical principles. I want to help them sow not a seed of corruption, but a seed of prevention. This is merely a wake up call. Too many pastors and religious leaders are encountering their children having sex before marriage. That's heartbreaking!

Our children and grandchildren, who were raised in a Christian home, thought that holding hands and innocent kissing wouldn't lead to such things as sexual explosion either. But it did! And too, they are good teenagers. There should be a support system for them to interact with other leaders with parental approval to curtail so many pregnancies and homosexual endeavors.

All of us have made careless mistakes, and like all concerned parents, you don't want your children to make the same mistakes in their innocence. This is what we call preventive measures! If all possible, we want teenagers to avoid the pitfalls. And we desire that they communicate with us. They feel at times that parents are the enemy. We are not the enemy, only caring parents who love their children. Parents want their children and teenagers to be well-informed.

EVERYTHING IS RIGHT WITH YOU

Most teenagers are inexperienced and adorable! They think they know a great deal, but usually they don't. Sometimes, they receive erroneous information concerning personal growth and development from peers who misread something from an unreliable person. Their best information comes from a parent or the Bible.

Parents, Jesus loves children, and often used them as illustrations of purity and goodness in His teachings. In Matthew 19, children were brought to Jesus that he might lay hands on them. The disciples rebuked those who brought the children. In verse 14, Jesus said, "Suffer little children, and forbid them not, to come unto me: for of such is the kingdom of heaven."

In verse 15, He put hands on them and blessed them; they make up the kingdom of heaven. In other words, children are special and important to Jesus.

He can't put hands on them presently, but His Word is available for every child and teenager. Through the Word, children, you can be touched by your parent's instructions. Follow them closely! You hear Jesus' voice through the manifested Word preached by your pastor. Receive his words and let them be applicable to your life.

You who are saved and living a life of controlled abstinence, we commend you for not being sexually active. There is nothing wrong with you because you are not sexually active. Everything is right with you. Keep your innocence, your high quality of living, until you complete school, attend college, and find employment. After marriage come sexual explosions, uncomplicated. Before marriage, sex is wrong according to Scripture. If the person loves you, he or she should wait until marriage. 1 Corinthians 6:9, 18-19 states, "Know ye not that the unrighteous shall not inherit the kingdom of God? Be not deceived: neither fornicators, nor idolaters, nor adulterers, nor effeminate, nor abusers of themselves with mankind. Nor thieves, nor covetous, nor drunkards, nor revilers, nor extortions, shall inherit the kingdom of God. Flee fornication. Every sin that a man doeth is without the body; but he that committeth fornication sinneth against his own body. What? Know ye not that your body is the temple of the Holy Ghost which is in you, which ye have of God, and ye are not your own?" 1 Corinthians 7:2 gives clarity: "Nevertheless, to avoid fornication, let every man have his own wife, and let every woman have her own husband."

FOOL THE VERY ELECT

Every male teenager knows that the teenage girl eventually wants to get married. A young man knows that a young woman needs a man who can and will provide for her. Women don't need a man who can produce a baby but doesn't have a good job. He has skills to satisfy you, but he doesn't know how to fill out an application for employment.

We are not discussing a man who works in the pharmaceutical market, experienced in the distribution of various drugs. He has to have a work history but one that is legitimate. He wears an identification badge, but it is a false documentation made from the computer. The computer can fool the very elect.

Young man, finish school. Then think about a relationship. For now, you need an education, not a baby. It's obvious that you want to be known as a man. But you are a child. After your eighteenth birthday, according to law you will be a man.

What kind of man will you be, one with no skills or means of supporting a baby? No offense, but producing a baby doesn't make you a man. Accountability and responsibility with character and integrity makes one a man. And too, caring about the young lady will create an atmosphere for her to fall in love with your willingness to complete high school and pursue your goals for college. If it is meant to be, you'll be together in the end.

There are many uneducated daddies, without a vision, a dream, or a plan for their children. Most of the time, those daddies are trying to see how many babies they can produce. Young people, you are too blessed to be stressed out about whether or not he or she cares. Care about yourself.

HAVING SEX DOESN'T PROVE ONE'S LOVE

Communities of concerned citizens and parents, encourage teenagers to stay young as long as they can. Promote education and support them as they become the best that they can be in the sight of their heavenly Father.

Young people, some friends will tell you that it is all right to fall in love at an early age and to prove it by having sex. Having sex does not prove one's love; it means that you have a burning desire to connect with another person.

WHY ME, I AM NOT ATTRACTIVE?

To provide evidence of this message, let me tell you about a young female teenager, Lois, who was sought after by one of the cutest boys at her high school. He sought her out among all those pretty girls to be with her. Lois thought, "Why me? I am not attractive." Still, she was excited to have someone like him wanting to be with her.

He was a perfect gentleman. He walked her to class carrying her books. They met at the football games, and he walked her home, tenderly grasping her hand. Lois was in hog heaven.

They talked about many things, and never did he try to take advantage of her. One day, he asked a scary question. "Can I come to your house?"

Without hesitation the answer was no. He could not come to her house. She wasn't permitted to have company. Daily, he asked the same question and received the same answer. What was it about that answer he didn't understand?

Then one day he stated, "I want to meet your mother." Lois literally had an anxiety attack. Was he crazy? Time and time again, she made it known that he couldn't meet her mother, nor could he come to her house. That wasn't possible.

But one particular day, the question was asked, and though she gripped her lips to say no, yes came out before she had the opportunity to talk it over with her mother.

They agreed that he was coming over that Thursday. Sure enough, he came to the house, rang the doorbell, and the girl asked him in. Her mother was standing at the entrance of the living room as they stood on the porch.

Lois was shaking, and her knees were knocking. Her mother and the young man were observing each other, waiting for her to introduce them. But she was seemingly stuck on dumb and parked on stupid. Words would not come out of her mouth. Slowly he stepped past her to introduce himself and ask her mother if it would be all right for him to date the daughter. To the girl's amazement, her mother agreed that he could come to the house to see her daughter. Her mother added, "She is a young lady; treat her respectfully."

The boy agreed and he treated the girl with much respect. He came to the house almost daily. They sat on the sofa, watched television, and studied together. Several months passed and he hadn't asked her to be intimate with him, not that she wanted him to ask for anything but a kiss or a sweet embrace.

Nonetheless, that November things changed. He came over one Tuesday night while her mother was in prayer meeting, and her hidden desire was answered. They kissed and he embraced her sweetly. Later in the month, they indulged in having sex. After it was over, he promised to be with her and to like her forever.

She believed him. Now, what do you expect from a seventeen-year-old who had been struggling to be loved by her deserted father? She thought she was ugly and dumb. Her brothers called her the Ugly Duckling, and her teachers confirmed her dumbness. Also, she did not know fully where babies came from, and she experienced the anatomy of sexual activities for the first time. She was happy that someone cared for her. Never in a million years did she think kissing and embracing would cause her to get pregnant. Clearly, they didn't do it. They only enhanced matrimonial contact without a license. Out of ignorance, it happened, the first time having sex! Bang, she was pregnant. Her entire life changed.

Lois was in her twelfth year of high school, and now she was pregnant. Her mother and the school guidance counselor had made preparations for her to attend Spelman College in Atlanta. Although she wanted to attend Bethune College in Daytona Beach, Florida, they had the last voice. However, their dreams for her and her own dream of attending college diminished at the outcome of her pregnancy.

One spring day, she was called into the office of the guidance counselor. As she walked in, there were two other girls present. And before them, the counselor asked, "Can I touch your stomach to see if you are pregnant?"

"Pregnant! No, you can't touch me," she nervously sobbed.

"These two girls allowed me to touch them, why not you?" she asked. Stunned by her behavior, the teenager said, "My mother told me to not let an adult lay a hand on me. You cannot touch me."

"You won't let me touch you? You need a doctor's slip stating that you are not pregnant." The counselor got up from her desk and proceeded to walk towards the student, explaining that she needed to touch her stomach to determine if she was pregnant. The teenager backed out of the office and left school devastated.

It was hard for her to understand that the same woman who filled out her paperwork for college and chose her to work in the counselor's office was thinking this way about her. She walked home, thinking from two perspectives. *Why does she think I am a bad girl? And how am I going to explain to my mother that the counselor thought I was pregnant?*

She cried all the way home. She couldn't wait to get there to tell her mother what the counselor said and tried to do to her. Mostly, she wanted her mother to go back to the school with her to give the counselor a piece of her mind.

As she approached the doorway of her home, she told her mother everything. Instead of going to the school, her mother sweetly said, "If you are pregnant, you are not the first girl to have a baby out of wedlock, and you will not be the last. I will support you through your pregnancy, but you will not have another baby until you are married."

Her mother's response was not to sanction sex; it was a defense mechanism because she didn't adequately teach, in the home, abstinence before marriage.

Sex is not acceptable prior to marriage. Teenage boys and girls should know that abstinence is the best policy for a Christian walk. Teens can be kept pure if they want to be kept by sufficient teaching and by the power of God. Young man or girl, there is nothing wrong with you if you are not sexually active. Remain there until marriage.

THE DOCTOR'S REPORT PROVED DIFFERENTLY

In the young girl's heart, she was angry with herself for violating her mother's trust. She never thought that the first time having sex would cause her to get pregnant. Frightened as she was to tell her mother, it was an easy transition. Her mother continued with this statement, "We will make an appointment with the doctor. That will determine the outcome, and let's take it from there. Too, if you are pregnant, we will deal with it."

That very same day, she saw her family doctor, and the test proved that she wasn't pregnant. The next day, when she took the report back to the school and gave it to the counselor, she went ballistic. She began to scream, "You can't attend this school pregnant! I don't care what the report says; you are pregnant. Another Nelson can't graduate pregnant, embarrassing the school. She leaped toward the teenager, fanning the report in her face and saying, "You have to go; you can't attend this school. You will be transferred."

Lois was discombobulated for a few moments. She was unaware of what the counselor meant. Then, it dawned on her. The counselor was talking about an incident with her brother Marc and his wife Mary.

Marc and Mary were seniors, embarking upon graduation. Marc was the principal leader of his class in scholarships. He received thirteen scholarships to attend various colleges. Because of his recognition for the scholarships, the local newspaper wanted to interview him and have him take pictures with the school principal. The principal was elated to have his picture taken with Marc, a student epitomizing greatness, from the prestigious New Stanton Senior High School in 1961.

However, there was a stipulation to the picture taking after Mary couldn't march with her class. Marc and Mary were married, but because she was expecting a baby she couldn't march with her class. She was able to get her diploma; she couldn't march with her graduating class. In Marc's head that wasn't fair. The rule stated that a pregnant girl could not march if her pregnancy were known.

Marc went to the principal to make him an offer that he couldn't refuse, and that decision was reversed. Marc returned home with her cap and gown. That evening they marched together. It was true that rules are capable of changing.

Two years later the family faced another situation. The teen's situation was different. Although the teen wasn't pregnant, she was being thrown out of school because of what Mary and Marc did. The girl's written proof stating that she wasn't pregnant wasn't good enough for the counselor.

The next month, she was sent to night school out of reach of her friends. She didn't believe she was pregnant. Her belief was in the doctor's report. He examined her and found nothing.

Her friends' parents didn't want them to associate with her. Throughout the community, she was known as a bad girl. Her brothers were embarrassed that their sister was pregnant. Before long, her stomach was big; shortly the baby moved. Quickly, she found that she was an immature child who performed an illegal adult act.

At this point she realized, *I am on the verge of having a baby and don't have a plan.* Her boyfriend wanted to get married before the baby was born, but she wasn't certain that she wanted a husband. She only wanted to be shown love.

The teenager understood that she was too young to take on the responsibility of a baby and a husband. She was really uncertain about the problem of her relationship to her boyfriend. Even though he kept his word to be by her side, she didn't know if she loved him, or whether he loved her enough to make her a good husband. She was so naïve about life, but she longed for a lasting relationship. She didn't want to leave him the same way her father deserted her, or for him to leave her.

My purpose for this illustration is to show young people that they don't need to have sex out of pressure to prove their love, or to demonstrate to their friends that they did the thing [the nasty]. I encourage them to do things God's way. God's way is for you to marry before having sex.

Marriage is honorable, but the bed is defiled [dishonored, unclean] before marriage. There are too many young girls who have babies and expect their parents [grandparents] to take care of them. This cycle can change if the curse is broken. Every community can band together to break the cycle. We command the curse of sexual activities before marriage to be broken off of our young people in Jesus' name.

I was married at a young age, and we didn't have anything to sustain us except our commitment to each other. We had children, and it was a struggle trying to adapt to both marriage and parenthood. We vowed to love, respect, protect, and watch over each other for better, for worse, for richer, for poorer, in sickness, and in health.

Although I didn't have proper training in being a wife or mother, I knew I could be my husband's lover and a mother to our children. I even knew what it meant to make a vow. A vow is a personal promise one makes with the intention of keeping it, a solemn pledge or oath to oneself or to another.

BOTH SIDES OF THE COIN

On either side of the coin is a head or a tail. On the heads side, all of us want someone to stand by our sides. I believed my husband would. Our vows were made with the hope that we would stay together for the rest of our lives, moving forward, making things better for our child. We were saved shortly after marriage. Together, we went to Sunday and mid-week services.

On the tails side, no matter how difficult it was financially, we purposed to keep our family together. My husband looked for a substantial job to provide for his family. He tried, seriously he did, but he couldn't find a good job with his limited education skills. Soon he found a job that required him to work late hours, which meant that the baby and I went to church alone.

We needed the support of both families. Even though they were there for us, we had to be accountable. We were one unit, our souls knitted, and we took advantage of our private moments. When I was pregnant with our second child, I felt a shifting in my spirit. Something was wrong in our marriage. At first, I thought it was the pregnancy, but it was more than the pregnancy. I could not pinpoint it, but things were changing with the happily ever after couple.

Even the fragrance of his cologne left swiftly. Where it used to linger, highlighting every room in the apartment, it was apparently racing to be in another location. His touch didn't have meaning. It didn't tell a story of how much pleasure I brought to his heart, that I was his sunshine in the rain, his calmness in the storm. His touch did not convey to me that I was his good thing. Something was drastically wrong, but I didn't know what. Later I found out that he was having an affair with another woman.

There is another side of the coin. Sometimes tails can be hard to swallow, when you know that you've done your best to please and to satisfy his every need.

DRIFTING AWAY LIKE THE WAVES

Never did I fully understand the power of submitting to my husband. Yet I wanted to have the benefits of submitting. I suppose that was what went wrong. I wanted to have the benefits rather than working for them.

Then, all I saw was him committing adultery and his strapping desire to fight me. It wasn't until three months after the birth of my son Sheldon that I knew for certain he had someone else.

After my arrival home from having our baby, I walked in the door knowing that someone had been in my home. That wasn't his skill, cleaning up. It was in my heart to ask for surety as to who maintained the apartment, but I didn't.

One morning I felt strong enough in my body to do some strenuous work. I wanted to flip our mattress. As I grabbed the mattress and slightly raised it, I saw a black pair of women's panties under the mattress. They were not mine. Of course, I was curious about to whom they belonged and how they got under the mattress. In my head, I could only think about the day I came home from the hospital with our son to find the house cleaned.

"How can he do this to me?" I tearfully murmured. "What is wrong with him? Where was his head? Is he mindless?" I couldn't wait until he came home to ask these questions. I prepared his meal as usual, ran his bath water, and had his clothes resting on the bed. I waited patiently to ask the important question and to see the look upon his face.

He came home as normal and kissed me on my cheek. Before he could hug me, I flashed those panties in his face and asked, "Who do these belong to?"

His eyes stretched as he stuttered, "That brother of mine. I'm going to get him. He had that woman in the house while we were gone."

I added, "How can that be, when I'm home at all times?"

"Honey," he spoke. "It perhaps was the time when you had the baby."

Loudly I yelled, "You mean to tell me that your brother had sex in our bed. He cannot come here anymore. He is not allowed in my house. That act was disrespectful. It was disrespectful of him to have another woman in our home. He is a married man, why have sex with another woman?"

He pulled me towards him and voiced, "I understand that you are hurt; I'm going to speak with him. You are right. That was disrespectful."

Deep down in my soul, I knew it wasn't his brother. It was him who had a woman in our dwelling place, our bed. It's no wonder his touch didn't feel as if I were his good thing. I wasn't his anymore; he moved someone else into that position. He was too calm in his actions. Normally, when angry, he walked the floor or smoked a cigarette outside. This time, he did nothing to illustrate his anger.

I couldn't prove it, but I felt it to be true in my heart that another woman was lurking around somewhere. From that day forward, I randomly asked, "Are you seeing someone else?"

Each time he answered the same words, "No, I don't have another woman." Although he spoke those words, his behavior demonstrated otherwise. The scent of another woman was present in his life. He dumped me for the affections of another person who caused him to occasionally spend the night away from home. He also provoked the situation by not paying the rent where his children rested their heads. He lied in so many ways about the other woman that it was disgraceful and painful.

Although we had been married for twenty-six months, he was too young and immature for marriage. He obviously thought that he was not so attached and committed in our relationship that he could not have another woman or multiple women.

I say to you what my grandmother said to me. Complete high school and attend college. Then get married and live happily ever after. There is no hurry to get involved with something for which you are not prepared. Take your time, seek God, and get to know yourself.

DISPLAY FAMILY VALUES

Our children are under so much pressure. There is pressure to succeed, to do right, to make good grades, and to get a good education. Within that pressure, we should teach our children to obey their parents in the Lord, for it is right. It is crucial that children honor their fathers and mothers, which is the first commandment with a promise, that it may go well with them and that they may enjoy long life on the earth (Ephesians 6:1-3).

I believe that if we change parenting strategies, they will do right, make good grades, and subsequently not be stressed. Our parenting skills come from our parents. We do not think about these skills, we automatically do them. Never do we think to judge whether their training was positive or negative unless a family member wakes up one morning, from being with God, with wisdom to state that our parents and we are wrong in our parenting technique, and we need to change. Change, breaking a long-established cycle, takes courage.

The best of parents make mistakes and treat children in a manner which needs to be reexamined. I made mistakes. I had to apologize to my sons for raising them in the wrong manner. Teaching them biblical principles of how to think and loving them were together. Not allowing them to express themselves was teaching them to accept any and everything. In part they were provoked, and they couldn't speak. It was hard for them to digest, and it was more difficult for me to change. But we did, and it brought us closer than ever before.

JUST SPEAK THE TRUTH

To the fathers the Scripture further states, "Do not provoke your children to wrath, but bring them up in the training and admonition of the Lord" (Ephesians 6:4).

Include your children in any decisions that affect changes in the home. They need to know what is happening. Without knowledge they sometimes think they are at fault for the downfall in the family, and a shift in personality and behavior takes place. We can avoid some things and keep down disturbance by letting children know that they are of value. As they ask questions, give them answers in meekness and fear. This does not take anything from you; it simply states that you are a doer of the Word. They may not agree with the answer, but they are included in the process of what decisions the family makes. Therefore, don't worry about frightening them, just speak the truth.

I recall troubles with one of my fifteen grandchildren, Renee. She was encouraged to be the best that she can be by her parents. They instructed her to achieve in life. But there were days when she didn't think she could achieve in life because of the mistakes she made. Too, she was at a cross road of indecision about wanting to live with her mother or with her father. They separated, and she was in the middle. At least she thought so. She would do small yet foolish things to see who would run to her rescue. To support her, both parents did!

At one point, Renee wanted to be with bad, rough boys with blemished representations. That behavior led her into a downward spiral. Thank God that didn't last.

She was abused by one parent and rescued by the other parent. She was a typical girl, looking for identity, wanting to be recognized for whom she was, and seeking love from both sides of the family. Yet in her search, she was ridiculed, deceived, and denied. One parent discouraged her by putting many demands on her, and the other parent encouraged her to continue moving forward to get an education. She could have given up, but she chose to press through the excruciating pain. She ultimately found herself, and soon will graduate from one of the local colleges in Jacksonville,

Florida. Hallelujah! She made it through a category three storm to reach the first phase of her destiny. When times got hard, she held on and pressed towards the mark. For her commitment, it's her time to succeed.

CHAPTER 7

I'm Single, Speak to Me!

I am many things to many people, but is there a word for me? I need a word to encourage me to move forth and not stand still while waiting for the right man or woman to hold me.

I am alone, but not lonely. I am employable and can't find a job. What word do you have for me? I am attractive. I have dreams and goals, but I don't want to be alone. Give me a word to encourage my soul.

My brother and my sister, there is a special word that teaches you to guard your heart and lean not to your own understanding. Let God direct your path as you build a relationship with Him, the Author and Finisher of your faith. The Word is: be enlightened by your inner self and know that you should not be touched until marriage. Be anxious for nothing to receive something. This is just for you, the single man or woman who trusts in the Lord.

*N*ot like teenagers, those of you who are mature with wisdom may want companionship in a more detailed manner. That companionship can be given by a friend for an evening escort to a special function where you will not be alone. Yet, with that concept, although justified, you still want to be loved. Also, a woman still wants to hold on to a man's strong yet gentle arms to escort her to numerous social and church functions. You don't always want him to be known as the next door neighbor. Think of times when you have felt like this! Your pulse quickens, you're perspiring with palms sweaty at the thought of being alone for an important event.

Your belief system is the basis of your expectation for a permanent relationship. Miracles still happen. You are in position for a miracle.

AWESOME, UNIQUE, AND BLESSED

One spring day as I spoke with Deloris on the matter of being single, she said to me, "All my life I knew I was different in my singleness, but I didn't understand the significance of it until I read Myles Munroe's book, *Single, Married, Separated, and Life After Divorce*."

Those words encouraged me to purchase the book. In chapter two, Munroe covers singleness. He writes, "Singleness is a state to be pursued, not avoided. To be single should be the goal of every married person."[1]

I thought to myself, *when you are married, you become one. But when does it happen?* As I pondered that thought, I realized that marriage is singleness, singleness of heart, mind, and soul.

Dr. Munroe continues, "The primary thing you need to understand from Scripture is that when God observed that it was not good for Adam to be alone, Adam was totally whole [Eve was taken out of him], totally unique, and totally separate. He did not even know he needed someone else!"[2]

In other words, God said that it is not good for a man to be alone if he is single. You do not need to marry someone until you are truly

---

1 Myles Munroe, *Single, Married, Separated, and Life After Divorce (New York: Books, 1989), p. ,17*
2 Munroe, p. 17

a single person. You are better off alone, if you are not yet single – if you are not yet unique, separate, and whole.

In reality, is Dr. Munroe saying that a woman needs to know without doubt that she is unique, separate and whole before marriage? If she does not, she will hurt someone. For that reason, when she knows she is awesome, unique, and blessed, she is a prime candidate for marriage.

Does this then mean that when a man seeks after a woman, he does not find his wife but a run of the mill woman who can be exploited? How frightening! Does that mean that when he finds a woman and goes to bed with her, he marries somebody else's wife before his wife is ever found? But when a man truly knows who he is and what he wants, he then finds a wife, his good thing. For this reason, a man has no business looking for a woman, but, when mature, he should find a wife. I recommend that we, who are unique, whole, and separate, express to every young adult the importance of singleness and the importance of being abstinent.

Unique is defined as special, unusually different. Whole is totally without blemish. Separate is the state of being apart from something that is not growing naturally.

Singleness can be a permanent position for those who don't want to get married. Or, it can be temporary for those who desire to get married. The difference is that one sect wants to be single and the other sect wants to get married. But in the meantime, the group who wants a husband will build a relationship.

SINGLE LIFE: FULFILLMENT IN THE WORD

In a recent single's conference, Dr. Eugene McCormick of the Florida Baptist Convention spoke on the five foundations for fulfillment in the Word. He stated that as singles seek to find fulfillment in the Word of God, their search should include the following activities.

1. Reading – Read expectantly and prayerfully. Reflect on the Word, building character with comprehension. Read to be blessed (Revelation 1:3).

2. Hearing – Hear with an attentive ear; faith in the Word comes by hearing. Hear with a special sensation. Most of us only do selective listening. After reading the Word, hearing it is important (Romans 10:17).

3. Studying – Study the Word; make it personal to create discipline. As you read, do it out loud. Don't just take what you read at face value, study to prove yourself strong in the Word (Acts 17:11).

4. Memorizing – Memorization of God's Word will generate a reservoir where, when needed, the Word will be automatic (Psalm 119:9, 11).

5. Mediating – Mediation is like spiritual digestion. God's Word sustains us (Psalm 1:2-3).[3]

A single life consists of having fulfillment in the Word. Every single person should seek after the things of God. Seeking a man or woman to bring fulfillment will be complete when you go after God and his righteousness.

Living a life in the spirit of righteousness draws righteous people together. The man, to whom God gave the charge to find a wife, will find a woman to be his wife as he equips himself spiritually and financially.

Dr. McCormick also said, "Living a life of total fulfillment is what God desires for all believers to experience. It doesn't matter whether one is black or white, rich or poor, learned or unlearned, married or single, living a life of fulfillment is a divinely ordained state. Jesus Christ himself declared in John 10:10b, 'I have come

3 Eugene McCormick, Dr, Jacksonville Baptist Association as African American Ministries Director "Single Life: Fulfillment in the Word" (Jacksonville, FL) March 25, 2006

that they might have life, and that they might have it more abundantly.' The Good News translation reads, 'I have come in order that you might have life – life in all its fullness.' However, living life in all its fullness requires submission to the terms set forth by Christ." Consider the following:

1) Singles must find their dependence in God's Word (Job 23:12; Matthew 4:4).

2) Singles must focus their delight in God's Word (Psalm 40:8; Psalm 145:19).

3) Singles must fix their devotion in God's Word (Joshua 1:8; Isaiah 58:2).

4) Singles must forge their destiny in God's Word (Psalm 37:23; Joshua 21:45).[4]

Single men and women, it is a blessing to focus your attention on the Master, fulfilling every requirement for a godly life. When you focus your attention on God, you will reap marvelous miracles and blessings. If you start right, you will end right.

If your motive is pure before engaging in a courtship with a man or woman, then your end will be pure. As you engage in a relationship correctly, you will treat that other person with the deepest respect. Your investment of time will be cautiously examined. Time should not be wasted. In essence, your time should be used wisely and not foolishly (Ephesians 5:15).

Be in a position at all times to redeem the time; be wise and understand what the will of the Lord is (v.18), being filled with the Spirit (v.19).

Living a Spirit-filled life does not prevent you from encountering catastrophes, failures, and difficult days. From one time period to another, married couples have days like these. The difference is that they have each other, but you singles have only the Lord with whom to communicate directly. He is more potent in communication than a

4 Dr. McCormick

spouse. At all times, He will be honest with you. The truth of God's Word must be in your view forever. Living in the state of holiness does not mean that you are weak or ignorant. It means that you are bold enough to overcome, while submitting to God, until you are married. Then you can submit yourself to your spouse in the fear of God.

CHAPTER 8

I Want to Get Married

*P*reparedness is the charge for marriage. Every woman wants to be married. In her heart, she wants to know the joy of marriage. Extenuating situations may have caused her to change her mind and to substitute single livelihood for a marriage.

Some times, settling for single living can be a cop out. It's obvious that we can accept something different if things don't work our way. To save face, we make substitutions and reasonable excuses!

A woman can prepare for marriage. But she can't get married until someone finds her. When he finds her, he finds a good thing. In your precious hearts, do you know that you are a good thing? Proverbs 18:22 states, "Whoso findeth a wife findeth a good thing, and obtaineth favor of the Lord."

Who is a good thing? A good thing can be a woman with property, education, wisdom, and insight to enhance the sanctity of marriage through love, and a woman who has a strong relationship with God.

Are you the Proverbs 31 woman? Her price is above rubies. Her husband will be able to trust her. She will do him good and not evil.

She is one who will cook and prepare a meal for her husband and children. Can you cook a real meal, not microwave meals? Can you really cook a healthy meal? A Proverbs 31 woman gives to the poor and provides for her husband. Will you work and take care of your husband emotionally and physically? Can you learn how to make your clothes and not shop, spending your money and his money so that the household goes lacking? Will you give him children who will rise up and call you blessed? Too, will he be able to call you blessed and praise your virtuous name? Are you that virtuous woman? Are you ready to put your needs and wishes on the back burner?

MARRIAGE IS MINISTRY

During the winter of 2003, my spiritual daughter Shana and I attended her cousin's funeral. We talked in generalities, making sweeping statements. One area dealt with relationships. The conversation was not serious that caused her to say, "I don't know if I want a husband. I have seen so much." She stopped. I waited for the conclusion, but she had finished the statement. A short while before, in Sunday morning worship service, I spoke on the subject of the power of submission that dealt with preparation for marriage. Maybe that service prompted the remark.

In my message, I told the congregation that because marriage was ministry, if they were not able to commit and obey, it didn't make sense to consider marriage. They were informed that marriage was sacred; it wasn't anything to with which to play. And if they chose people who were unequally yoked, they should be willing to accept them as they were instead of trying to change them after marriage. Then, as they grew spiritual and understood the importance of being unequally yoked, they should consider whether they were able to wait for the manifestation of holiness to come. Could they give their body when their spouse wants it in view of the fact that after marriage, your body no longer belongs to you. It cannot be refused.

For a moment, the church was quiet. My mission was to make sure those women and men understood that marriage is ministry. Both are serious, and can be fulfilling and rewarding when taken sincerely. Personally speaking, I believe that the way a person is before marriage is the way he or she remains, unless that person is serious about making godly changes.

It is the same way with salvation. A person who was over-weight, slim and trim, or silly before being saved, would still be that way after salvation.

Prayerfully, Shana didn't make the statement because she feels time is a factor and marriage is not in her view. She is thirty-eight with two children from a previous marriage. The devil may be trying to plant a seed thought that she will not get married and that her life should be spent with God and God alone. Well, at this time, if those thoughts exist she should have her mind directly on God, building intimacy with Him, so when her husband does come, she'll know how to minister to him as God ministers to her. I am certain that she will get married. She is a beautiful woman whom God has cleansed; He is restoring and rebuilding her. As she releases all the hurt and pain from previous relationships that contaminated her flesh and spirit, God is filling her with goodness.

When God completes the work in her, she will not transfer anything into her marriage that reminds her of another man. God is purifying her and getting her prepared for His glory.

In Temple of Light Fellowship Ministries, it is our custom to encourage men and women to keep themselves until marriage. The Bible states that a man should not touch (1 Corinthians 7:1) a woman sexually before marriage. Marriage is honorable, good, and praise-worthy. "Marriage is honorable among all, and the bed undefiled; but fornicators and adulterers God will judge" Hebrews 13:3-4).

SEXUAL ACTIVITIES PRIOR TO MARRIAGE

The point I'm about to make involves a serious situation that happened between an engaged couple, David and Gloria, who formerly attended our local fellowship. They got engaged and sought counseling from my mother, Pastor Louise B. Nelson, who was the pastor at that time. During counseling, my mother explained the importance of not engaging in sexual activities prior to marriage.

She told them that sexual intercourse is part of God's first command for husband and wife (Genesis 1: 28). Because they were not married they shouldn't be intimate with each other. Of course, they agreed. She continued, "Do not have sex, because on the day you marry I am going to ask about purity in front of the congregation. Also, if you are having sex, please abstain. The Lord is saying, 'When you have sex you will not get married.'"

They assured her that they were not. A few weeks later, David said to his fiancée, "We can be intimate now that we are engaged. We are getting married next month; nothing can happen." Gloria told me that she didn't want to indulge but agreed with him. The next day, the prophetic word from God materialized. David was belligerent towards Gloria. His personality changed to the point that he hated her. He called off the wedding and six months later married a woman he recently called "the woman from hell."

David wants to get out of the marriage, but his wife will not release him. She is in a backslidden state; she is not intimate with him. Before marriage she gave her money and body freely. But now she will not allow him to have free course of "his" body or "her" money.

She freezes up, and David says he's satisfied. Listen carefully to this: a satisfied man without sex is a grievous spirit. So you know that he is not being real. He is hurting, and pride tells him that he's okay.

FOLLOW DIRECTIONS

Men should have some essential information before they venture into an intimate relationship. First, know the woman. David knew Gloria, but they did not follow directions. He violated a law and then married another woman, whom he didn't know. She gave him what she wanted until they were married. Later into the marriage, she began to find fault with his inability to be affectionate. She wanted more, and she went out and got it. And she presumed her husband should be happy about that move.

If any man wants to know the makeup of a woman, he should introduce her to his mother and sister. From one woman to another, they will let you know if she is for real or if she is a schemer. Too, give her several assignments to see if she will follow directions. Observe every aspect of your woman. A man's intent for being in a relationship should be marriage. If not, do not enter into a relationship hoping for sexual desires to be fulfilled.

THE LORD SAID UNTO THE WOMAN

The woman, Eve, sinned and brought transgression to the house. Genesis 3:13 states that after the woman obeyed the serpent, God spoke. "And the LORD God said unto the woman, what is this that thou hast done? And the woman said, the serpent beguiled me, and I did eat. Unto the woman he said, I will greatly multiply thy sorrow and thy conception; in sorrow thou shalt bring forth children; and thy desire shall be to thy husband, and he shall rule over thee."

To paraphrase, He said, "I will multiply, greatly multiply, your sorrow. You will become pregnant, and in childbearing there will be suffering and much pain. Because of your disobedience, you will have a yearning desire to your husband, and he shall rule over you."

Before a man touches a woman, he should obtain information about her character. Who is she? Is she a born again, mature Christian? He should know if she is a brawler after she drinks wine or beer. He should understand before marriage if he is going to have a gossiper, an abuser of words, or an intimidator in sexual matters.

Let's be real. Marriage should have boundaries. Every man and woman should be sober minded in marriage. It's more than being sexual. He must find out if she can wait until marriage, or if she wants him to indulge before he purchases the marriage license? Get to know one another. There is no hurry. You would hate to get up with a smile on your face to find him or her rushing to put on clothes and to get out of your house with the purpose of not ever returning any of your calls.

Before marriage, a man should discuss with the woman how he wants her to function in the home and away from the home. This is going to hurt, but he should have the option of choosing her friends.

Some things should be established before marriage. This is why it is important to have several months of counseling sessions before marriage. He needs to know if she is going to be a virtuous woman or a dreadful wife. A virtuous woman is an upright woman. "She does him good and not evil all the days of her life. She also rises while it is yet night, and provides food for her household. Strength and honor are her clothing; she shall rejoice in time to come. She opens her mouth with wisdom, and on her tongue is the law of kindness. She watches over the ways of her household, and does not eat the bread of idleness. Her children rise up and call her blessed; her husband shall praise her" (Proverbs 31:12-28).

Before Bishop and I were married twenty-five years ago, we talked for many hours about our lives [the hurts, pains, mistakes, and disappointments]. We also discussed what we expected from our friendship and marriage.

SINGLE WOMEN, PREPARE YOUR HEARTS

Marriage is a beautiful union, and every woman who desires to marry should do so. However, I plead with you not to reject marriage because you haven't been found. Your day will come. God has heard your cry and pitied your every groan for a godly relationship.

Single women, there is no other way to prepare your heart but to study the Word of God and to follow the instructions and teaching of your leaders. At times it may be hard to live a life of singleness. As you know, at times it is easy to get lonely, depressed and bored. But God sent His Word. You who are lonely, loneliness is merely a feeling of sadness which causes depression. Depression is a place of gloominess or having low fortitude. Sometimes loneliness causes single women and men to get attached to someone with good character. An individual with good character who does not have a personal relationship with God is troubled and dangerous. His split personality suggests potential unkindness, extreme jealousy, or unbearable hatefulness.

Those who are bored have negative thoughts derived from an inadequate behavior of not being able to conquer, or achieve things for God. In fact, they are tired of waiting, and they begin to make decisions and changes from a lonely heart.

Feelings of being lonely, depressed, and bored are expressed as behaviors. When a desire is not met, a person may deny the desire and shut off other desires. Preventing ever being hurt again, they create a safety net called psychological harmony. Psychological harmony is a process of expressing unity while hurting, and not showing any type of emotion of the present pain.

Separation from the existence of these feelings means grief. Grief, in relationship to not being married, will bring sadness and anger. However, for you God sent His Word: word of life, joy, and contentment.

The reason it is easy for single women to get lonely is that they think about that special day when they will be together with the man of their dreams to attend a movie, go to a restaurant, take walks on the beach, or have comforting moments of embracing one another. They attend weddings, wishing it were them walking down the aisle. Some things you must back away from, and weddings may be one of them.

And for these reasons alone, single women ought to prepare their hearts in Scripture and too obey the guidance of the watchman of their souls. If they don't take heed to given instructions, they'll continue to do things their way. Their frustration and aggravation can develop into depression.

Depression is the tendency to lose hope and energy to embrace life at its fullness. In general, failures in life can cause depression. And when a man leaves without giving a valid reason for breaking up with a woman, he makes matters worse. She begins to feel as though she will never be able to embrace true love or marry the man of her dreams. For certain, the man who left may not be the man of her dreams.

Anyway, a woman also began to think that life and everyone else has let her down and that nobody loves her, in the vein of how she pours her heart into another person. She cries herself to sleep, won't eat for days, won't comb her hair, won't dress up, and won't take regular baths. Washing off is good enough. Incorrect, this is not the right comeback to a severe dilemma. Women! Washing off is not the answer.

Single women, you sometimes find yourself in a state of depression, and you can't find a way to pick yourself back up again. All of this could have been avoided if you were equipped to love yourself and definitely love God who created you.

As soon as you begin to think of yourself as a prize that can never be bought, you see the beauty in which you are and the true purpose for living. When you prepare your heart, focus on God, and obey your leaders, you will not have so much time to concentrate on boredom.

Being bored causes you to seek after negative things that may or may not produce destruction in your life. Boredom will cause you to sleep with different partners, floating in all of the wrong beds and turning into something that you didn't ever want to become: for example, tampering with drugs, alcohol, nicotine, marijuana, and many other substances. One may turn against the Word of God and hear words that give them acceptance. Changing bed partners does not always means sleeping from one woman or from one man to another. You can be in bed with the wrong person when you take on their mannerisms, their concepts, and their beliefs. You begin to lean to their understanding and fade away from God's love.

Boredom can cause you to celebrate all night and wake up from your sleep in a bed occupied by strangers. Boredom is a sure way to pierce hell. That's why the Bible states, "And withal they learn to be idle, wandering bout from house to house" (1 Timothy 5:13). To some, hell's damnation of the soul is not worth this behavior. The Spirit within forbids that you neglect the Word, which will heal, deliver, and set free.

KNOW THE RIGHT MOTIVE TO HELP

Holy women who are making preparation for marriage, while you are getting ready, make sure your prayer is not to have a husband like King Ahasuerus: one who will get drunk, desire to share you with other men, and give you a letter of divorcement when you refuse.

In the Book of Esther is written the story of the removal of Queen Vashti. Queen Vashti was beautiful and fair to look upon. In the third year of her husband's, King Ahasuerus's, reign, he had a feast with various princes and his servants, showing off his wealth and his glorious kingdom. He commanded every man of power to do as he pleased.

Even Queen Vashti socialized with the women in the royal house. The men were drinking and being merry. Then, on the seventh day of the feast, King Ahasuerus appointed officers to get Queen Vashti to come where he was with the other men to show off her beauty. She refused to appear in his chamber, and he was angry and very wroth.

Vashti's name signifies beautiful (Esther 1:9). Yet while drunk with wine, the king wants her to parade herself half-dressed for him and other men to enjoy. She was made for him, not for the other leading men. In his condition, if anything had gotten out of hand, he was not able to protect his wife. Even though her body was created for him, it also belongs to God. The body is not meant for sexual immorality, but for the Lord, and the Lord for the body (1 Corinthians 6:13).

She well knew that this act of disobedience would cost her crown, if not her life. But she refused to come. Surely, everything considered, we have few women like Vashti. For some of the highest of the land will dress and deck themselves with the utmost splendor, even to the selvedge of their fortunes, to exhibit themselves nearly half naked at balls, plays, galas, operas, and public assemblies of all kinds, that they may be seen and admired of men, and even, to the endless reproach and broad suspicion of their honor and chastity, figure away in masquerades!

Vashti must be considered at the top of her gender. But Queen Vashti refused to come at the king's command by his chamberlains. Therefore the king was very wroth, and his anger burned in him. Her courage was equal to her modesty; she would resist the royal mandate rather than violate the rules of chaste decorum.

When she didn't appear, it became obvious that other women might demonstrate that same behavior. Something must be done. This kind of behavior must be eradicated immediately. The king said to the wise men, "What should we do?" They suggested that the king have a written command that Queen Vashti would never come before him again and that her royal estate be given to another woman better than she (Esther 1:9-22).

From a human sense, King Ahasuerus was wrong for his drunken behavior. In the spiritual realm, God chose Vashti to execute His plan so Esther could be the next queen. God also knew that Vashti would not submit to taking off her clothes in front of those other men. She understood the principle of her body belonging to her husband and her husband alone.

Some theologians think that she was disobedient to the king. I contend that God knew her character. He knew how the king was going to respond. Some even say that her beauty was no longer important. But she disgraced and embarrassed the king, and for that reason, she had to go.

Queen Vashti became a victim of her own beauty. She refused to violate herself by displaying before those men. All women should understand that Queen Vashti demonstrated that she had morality, principles, and integrity.

In today's society, beauty must come from within, having meaning and purpose that is not only shown outwardly, that would eventually achieve death inwardly.

Single women, while you are waiting, prepare your heart for your husband. When he does find you, salvation will be brought to the marriage with pleasure and peace. You'll have the ability to pray, travail, and walk in obedience with sanctification of the Spirit operating in your life. You must live a holy life in all manner of conversation (1 Peter 1:15).

If you are a person who has patience and a good understanding of who you want, perhaps you are ready to enter the doorway to a fulfilling journey of marriage with another person. You must know who you are and what your capabilities are before marriage.

A MAN WHO KNOWS WHAT HE WANTS

Before getting engaged, my son Sheldon came to talk with me about his decision. He spoke candidly. "Betty, I believe I am ready for marriage."

I was happy but I presented a crucial question to him. I asked, "Son, are you sure you have found your good thing? A wife is a good thing. If you are sure, then you are ready for marriage."

He replied, "Yes ma'am, I believe I am ready." Linda and Sheldon have been married for fourteen years, the year of deliverance and salvation!

From a biblical perspective, fourteen epitomizes Jacob and Rachel. They met at the well, watering sheep. Jacob looked upon Rachel, kissed her, lifted his voice, and wept (Genesis 29:11). After the kiss, he told her who he was. She ran to get her father Laban, who was Jacob's mother's brother.

As Laban saw Jacob, he said to him, "Surely you are my bone and my flesh." And Jacob stayed with Laban for a month. Laban said unto Jacob, "Because you are my brother, will you serve me for nothing? Tell me what your wages should be?"

Jacob fell in love with Rachel, and he said to Laban, "I will serve you seven years for Rachel, your younger daughter."

Her father said, "It is better that I give her to you than to give her to another man."

Jacob served seven years for Rachel. His love was so awesome that the years seemed like a few days for the love he had for her. At the end of the seven years, Jacob said unto Laban, "Give me my wife, for my days are fulfilled, that I may go in [have sex] with her."

Laban gathered together all the men in one place and made a feast. In the evening, he took Leah, his tender-eyed daughter, and brought her to Jacob, and Jacob went in unto her. Laban tricked Jacob and gave him Leah, the oldest daughter, for his wife. The morning following the wedding, Jacob found Leah with him and not Rachel. He said to Laban, "What have you done? Didn't I serve you seven years for Rachel?"

He was beguiled, and Laban said, "It must not be so in our country to give the younger daughter before the firstborn. Fulfill her week, and we will give you this also for the service which you shall serve with me seven more years." Jacob agreed. And Rachel was also given to be his wife.

A man who knows what he wants will do anything to get what he asks. In Jacob's situation, he loved Rachel. For his commitment to Laban, he gained more than what he asked. He received exceedingly above all that he asked or thought (Ephesians 3:20). He possessed Leah, Rachel, and their handmaids, who bore him children. What a remarkable narrative! We are not condoning arranged marriages, but they were common in that era (Genesis 29:11-30).

Sheldon knew in his heart that he wanted Linda. He forsook all others and married his good thing. She has proven to be a good and faithful wife, and he is dedicated to supplying her needs.

Women must know that they are ready and prepared for ministry. Ministry is when you are ready to pray, protecting your husband from the negativity of those who remember his past and refuse to move forward, thinking he can't change. Ministry is when you are prepared to deny family members the opportunity to critique him, seeing if he is fit for you. You must announce to the family that he is your husband, you love him, and you don't need the drama. Furthermore, they are not going to see what you see in him anyway. You must take a stand for your man!

Marriage is when you can strive to snatch him out of the hand of the enemy, who wants to destroy the respect he has for you. Let your marriage be held in high honor, in all things, as you build a highly favored marriage. It is a partnership of two people working together, building a foundation of togetherness. Marriage is conceived through love, not how much someone has to support your addictions to having more than someone else, out-dressing everyone you know, flashing money around, and living above your means. What you bring to the marriage is much greater than silver and gold. You bring an awesome woman with wisdom, grace, and insight.

If by chance you are powerful enough to surrender control and maintain dignity, you are again prepared for the journey of a lifetime in marriage. When you marry, you as a wife are to be in subjection to your own husband, even as Sarah obeyed Abraham, calling him lord.

A man who knows what he wants will go after it with his whole heart. A husband after marriage, likewise, must dwell with his wife according to knowledge, giving honor unto her as the weaker vessel. Make her feel like a needed woman, who can and will satisfy your needs.

All men know that a woman loves to talk. Talk to her, and listen with patience. Never ignore her; doing so will create great problems that are worse than her taking off her clothes in front of other men. To her, that may be a simple act if it will get your attention for regular conversations.

BACK AWAY FROM HIM

Growing up in the sixties, the girls I knew wanted a boy who was tall, dark, and handsome. They soon grew out of that. They realized that they wanted a man who would respect and provide for his family.

I'm not trying to discourage you from marriage, or from tall, dark, and handsome men. I don't want you to get a man who looks good but lives riotously and with whom you are involved only because you want things. If you are a saved single woman, you need a saved husband who loves God. Seeking after things will give you self-gratification for a moment.

Love is everlasting.

Think for a moment; are you running him down to get things? Are you sometimes frustrated and disturbed about his behavior? You might say, "I am not in a situation like this." Perhaps not, but is your male companion living a life of righteousness where he can teach you the Word of God? I realize he doesn't have to live a righteous life to speak the Word. However, it is important that he knows Jesus as his personal Savior and Friend while articulating God's Word. Head knowledge is great in its place, but can he help you when you are dying spiritually? He can speak intellectual rhetoric, but what about speaking life to your soul? Is he living with the negative behavior of thinking that he knows everything and he can't be taught anything?

Also, in your heart do you feel that an unrecognizable change is taking place? Do you perceive that this is not the time for you to marry? Do you sense that he isn't ready for marriage? If there is an ounce of hesitation, you should consider backing away from him. Disassociate from that person and the situation! You may want to move on, but you think that you can't. Yes you can. Take one foot, put it in front of the other, and move forward. Get out of his way. If his love is greater than him having a pity party and being selfish, he will come for you when he is matured. Then the question is whether you will be in position to take him back.

GET CONNECTED TO JESUS

Think about this for a moment. Who are your associates? Who introduced you to him? Why have you given him power over you?

Now, this is only an observation. A single woman shouldn't get emotionally involved with a man who is talking about living a single life while she is thinking marriage. The two attitudes don't measure up in wisdom. This is not meant to sound negative, but you need to see the real picture.

He told you before you got deeply involved that he didn't want to get married, and silently you believe you can change his mind. Stop the madness. Get connected to Jesus. Leave him alone! He is sincere with his words. He is actually telling you, "I don't want you for a wife. You are okay for a friend but not good enough to be my wife."

At this point, you need to ask the Holy Ghost to fall fresh on you. Another dip may be required. Get yourself out of bondage.

FROM THE COMMENCEMENT OF THEIR COURTSHIP

Last year, a beautiful woman came to the church for counseling. She was in her twenties and had been dating a young man for ten years. He told her from the commencement of their courtship that he wasn't in a situation to marry her. But she thought she could change his mind. For ten years she tried to make him give up his devotion towards his children to marry her. He was wrapped up in his children because he was still in love with his ex-wife. The young woman did all she could to make him marry her, and she wanted to know what to do. She asked, "Am I wasting my time?"

I wanted to say, "Enthusiastically 'yes'! You have been for ten long years."

He had already told her what to do. He exclaimed, "I am committed to my children. I don't want to get married." That statement was an indication to back away. He wasn't ready for marriage. His priorities were his children. Sometimes, all you need to do is to listen, and the other person will answer your questions and solve your problem. Although it was ten years later, she finally heard the clock ticking. It was painful but she moved on.

Recently, I heard that she was engaged to her ex-boyfriend. I could see myself in this situation, marrying out of spite. How dangerous! She didn't love her fiancée. Her heart was still with the other man. But her goal was to get married.

I recall an incident thirty-seven years ago of a young couple who were desperately in love with each other. They did everything together. She drove his car, cashed his paycheck, paid his bills, and kept some money for herself. He promised to marry her when his divorce was finalized. But he wasn't responsible enough to marry her when she told him they were expecting a baby. He told his parents that the woman was pregnant, and they packed his things and sent him to Detroit to live with a distant relative.

The woman didn't see him until six years later. He came back to town to see her, and he made the announcement that because he was going to be a Baptist minister, he needed a wife. The amazing thing was that he was willing to tell her that he needed a wife, but it wasn't her he wanted. He could be a preacher and a husband, but not a father to his six year old son. His coming back, she thought, was to give support to their son. He didn't volunteer to pay child support, nor did he give her any type of support for the child. And she didn't take him to court.

After twenty-five years of being a pastor, he got word to his son that he wanted to meet him. The son lived for thirty-one years without a father; now the father wanted to be a responsible parent. That woman was infuriated, and she searched the city until she found him. When they met, she asked, "Why now? What do you want with my son?"

He replied, "I have been sick and I need to know my son."

She nervously spoke. "Where were you when he needed you? When he was sick, you didn't come or call. He needed to talk, and you were not available. So now you want to build a relationship with my son?"

He said, "I heard how well you raised him. I want to get to know my son. My other sons are away from the city, and I don't know how long I have."

"That is rubbish!" she said.

The man's interpretation of fatherhood was to confuse his son about life and to tell him that all men need two or more women. All those years he waited to have a relationship with his son to impart rubbish. "One woman is not enough to sustain you," he told his son. This come back father had the nerve to give this advice to his son. What does this tell you? A call is without repentance. Psalm 1:1 tells us, "Blessed is the man who does not walk in the counsel of the wicked or stand in the way of sinners or sit in the seat of mockers" (NIV). Where was he sitting when he told his son, "One woman can't satisfy a man?" He sowed an unfruitful seed in his son's spirit, and it appeared that the son believed his father.

The young man should have been more alert. He should have not believed his father. His mother and grandmother were his spiritual leaders. They taught him the Word of God. He knew what was right and what was wrong.

I suppose he was gullible for love and acceptance; furthermore, he acknowledged his father's word as truth. There is a possibility that his father's entrance into his life brought out what was already in him. My sister-in-law, Cherlynette, always says, "What's in you will come out." I suppose it did.

AN UNGODLY SEED

The son was a charming person, and it was easy for women to fall prey to him. This young, articulate man received an ungodly seed into his spirit, and he was trying to amuse himself on weak women.

As a small child, maybe nobody stressed to him that he was truly loved. Who could really say why a person does what he does? Well, we understand that there is an enemy who desires to sift you like wheat.

Perhaps, you weren't told, "I love you." Perhaps you heard, "You will never be anything. You are just like your father or mother."

Recently, you may have found someone to give you what you longed for. You longed to hear, "I love you." Even if those words are lies, lies sound truthful to a vulnerable person and will fulfill several voids. Maybe you are drawn to the words, not the man. Men are usually thought of as being pointless in certain areas. But they study women more than we think. They can look through you, see what you want, and give you what you desire. If you want attention and love, it can be arranged swiftly.

That young man was in a non-sexual relationship with one woman, but he quickly moved in with another woman and lived with her for several years before his main woman caught up with him.

The first woman was devoted to him, just as faithful as most wives. She was concerned about his daily living; she made sure he ate, put clothes in the cleaners, and paid his bills. She knew him better than his parents. After he was exposed, she wanted him more than ever.

A FOOLISH SCENARIO

Just suppose he wasn't caught by being seen with the other woman, but exposed while the first woman and the live-in woman were standing in the tax collector's office paying a particular bill for him. Suddenly the two women's eyes meet. The live-in woman gets out of line to say to the first woman, "It's amazing seeing you here. Why are you here?"

The first woman states, "I'm paying Terrance's water bill. Why are you here?"

The second woman says, "That can't be so. The water bill is paid; I am getting ready to pay his light bill. You are living in a dream world. You need to get over him. He is my man."

Before either woman calls to confront him, they take care of the water and light bills. Where is the elevator? The live-in woman calls him; the other woman goes to his workplace. She arrives at the pivotal point to overhear him talking to the live-in woman on the phone. He states that the first woman, who is now outside his office, wasn't there to pay his bill. "She was lying, and you should not have bought into that. She is angry that we are together."

The first woman stands at his desk, gazing at him, one brick short of a load, as he ignores her or perhaps pretends that he doesn't see her while he makes amends with the other woman. This is a foolish scenario. But this could have happened somewhere in the world. Hopefully, this doesn't fit you.

SHE BROKE HIS HEART

The first woman had a plan. Even though he moved out, she was still determined to get him back. Well, at least that is how it appeared. The young appealing man's father told him that he needed more than one woman to satisfy him. The first woman reflected on the time when her mother told her to stay one up on a man.

She continued to serve him; yet in her mind she was determined to break his heart. Love had now turned to hateful revenge. Sure enough, she broke his heart by having another man on the side. He understood her and could read her, but he didn't compute that piece of data. Her family was involved in her plan of trickery. They knew she had another man and thought it was amusing. That wasn't funny; it was dangerous.

One winter night he went to her house, only to find that she and the new boyfriend were leaving to attend a movie. He found out that night that she always had him on the side, just in case. You know the just in case situations: just in case he dumps her, she can fall back on the other man. Just in case she has enough of him, she can move safely into another relationship as if the new man were the first.

What a waste it was for them to play games. Ten years of another person's life was gone down the drain because two people chose to play intellectual games. The devil is a liar!

She eventually married. But he is still living single, trying to heal and recapture the joy of the Lord that he allowed the devil, through his father's disastrous words, "You need more than one woman," to use to separate him from God.

He understands that he needs His heavenly Father who was with him always, not his biological father who deserted him and didn't know enough about him to help guard his heart. Although the father was a minister, he gave entrance to the devil to destroy lives and relationships. In his own marriage, he left his wife to marry another woman. What will happen to the new wife? Keep her in your prayers.

CHAPTER 9

Building a Powerful Marriage

Submitting yourselves one to another in the fear of God. Wives, submit yourselves unto your own husbands, as unto the Lord. For the husband is the head of the wife, even as Christ is the head of the church: and he is the saviour of the body. Therefore as the church is subject unto Christ, so let the wives be to their own husbands in every thing. Husbands, love your wives, even as Christ also loved the church, and gave himself for it; That he might sanctify and cleanse it with the washing of water by the word, That he might present it to himself a glorious church, not having spot, or wrinkle, or any such thing; but that it should be holy and without blemish. So ought men to love their wives as their own bodies. He that loveth his wife loveth himself. For no man ever yet hated his own flesh; but nourisheth and cherisheth it, even as the Lord the church: For we are members of his body, of his flesh, and of his bones. For this cause shall a man leave his father and mother, and shall be joined unto his wife, and they two shall be one flesh. This is a great mystery: but I speak concerning Christ and the church. Nevertheless let every one of you in particular so love his wife even as himself; and the wife see that she reverence her husband.

Ephesians 5:21-33

*M*y husband introduces this message to married couples and to those who come for premarital counseling. The secret of building a strong marriage is for both spouses to recognize that they are servants. They serve the needs of each other. They are to love, respect, communicate, and submit. It's necessary for her to listen to him, and for him to listen to her.

Keeping our mouths closed and ears open can be troublesome at times, especially if you were like me growing up. My mother's philosophy was that children are to be seen and not heard. Now that I am delivered from bondage, freedom is upon me and it's hard not to speak an opinion based on truth. Even in truth and deliverance, there is a need for insight. Maybe by now we should have learned when to keep our lips together and thoughts to ourselves.

Within the boundaries of building a powerful marriage it takes love. Love is a deep sincere devotion for another person. Love will bring out the best in us.

Life is for those who abide in the beauty of holiness, doing the will of God. He gave permission for us to be fruitful and multiply. No matter when you got married, the decision to spend quality time together was established. From that point, you wanted to be together for the rest of your lives. "For that reason, the man left his father and mother to cleave [unite] to his wife. You are no longer two, but one flesh. Therefore, what God has joined together, let no man separate" (Matthew 19:5-6).

God ordained marriage, and He ordained the bed for man and woman to enjoy. As the ordained bed is spent by you and your husband, avoid conflict by being consistent in satisfying him and loving it. In the bed, there is an opportunity to resolve conflicts, problems, or tribulations by speaking the language he loves.

EXPRESS YOURSELF

Now is the time for you to enjoy sexual gratification. As often as possible, engage in sexual activities. Forget the other garbage, and unite in the bedroom. There are some exceptions to the rule. You could be unable to engage in sexual activities due to medical reasons, job duties, or military obligations. Other than that, express yourself. Doing so makes a healthy marriage. Demonstrate your love to each other.

I know what you are thinking. This book is about sex. That's all she is talking about. No, not true, it's also about your getting rid of those aches: the headache, eye ache, backache, leg ache, earache, stomach ache, butt ache, and knee ache so that you can concentrate on the real issue, to build a strong marriage. You are constipated with aches. Take a spiritual bath. Until you get a release, you can't satisfy yourself or anyone else. You are bound to less important matters.

To better assist you, I'll tell you of my out-of-order experience with Herb. I waited thirteen years for him to find me. I knew when we got married that we loved each other, but I didn't think I had to let him know my every move. I didn't think I had to ask permission to go to the shopping mall or visit my girlfriends. On Saturdays, I thought I had free course to do what I wanted. Before leaving home, I made sure he was fed and other needs were met. I didn't see any harm in what I was doing. As long as his needs were met, I could go and stay as long as I wanted.

All of that ended one weekend twenty-five years ago. Herb confronted me as I approached the front door. He asked in a soft tone, "Where are you going?"

I said, "Shopping with a friend."

He replied, "Did you forget something?"

In my mind, I knew that everything was done, and in all honesty I couldn't think of anything that was omitted.

He continued with, "Did you forget you have a husband? You can't continue to leave me in the house without asking me to go with you. Sometimes you leave home without saying a word. How long is this going to continue? You need to ask me if you can go."

I was shocked at his statement. Actually, I was offended. I thought to myself, *what does he mean, I need permission. I am a grown woman; I can do what I want.* I didn't speak it out loud for him to hear. I only thought those strong words.

Suddenly, the Holy Spirit quickened my spirit with these words, "You must obey your husband. You must also respect him as being the head of his wife."

I listened to the Spirit of God as He spoke those words. Immediately, I realized I was wrong. His voice penetrated in the same way it did when I prayed for the young man with the headache. I hurriedly asked my husband's forgiveness.

Why couldn't I have realized my behavior was wrong before God brought it to my attention? I suppose it was because this wasn't taught to me. Is that really the answer for justifying my behavior? Carefully, I began to look at marriage and its responsibilities. I also took a look at what I was doing and thought, *I don't want him to leave me in the house all day while he visits friends.*

I was so excited about being married that I forgot to give respect. I understood that when I heard God and obeyed Herb, from that moment, order was formed, then, blessings. I learned that Herb didn't want me to get permission. He wanted to be included in my plans. He wanted us to plan our weekends as we planned and arranged our debts, together. We communicated optimistically to get a clear understanding of what was wrong. I apologized and gave him a big hug. We have never had that misunderstanding again.

From that point, I began to adorn him with respect and honor. He and I enjoyed those Saturdays together by getting to know each other.

Ask yourself these questions. Do you want your husband to receive from you? Do you want him to respect and respond positively to your conversation? Well, you need to talk with your husband. Apologize and ask him for forgiveness. You may not have done anything wrong, but you should still apologize.

1 Peter 3:1 states, "Likewise, ye wives, be in subjection to your own husbands; that, if any obey not the words, they also may without the word be won by the conversation of the wives; while they behold your chaste conversation coupled with fear."

Peter, an apostle of Jesus Christ, gives advice to wives to be modest, respectful, and humble towards their husbands. To the wives he further states, "be in subjection, subdue, and submit to the obedience of your own husbands" (1 Peter 3:5).

This is a hard pill to swallow. I know it is. It was difficult for me to comprehend this message, coming from a man's perspective. Obedience can be a hard pill to swallow, especially when you don't know the full definition and how great the blessings can be. Obedience is better than sacrifice. We must be consistent in giving honor and respect as we receive many blessings. There are many blessings for us through obedience.

In Peter's writing there is an underlying code. I never gave it much attention, but when I saw it, I was blown away. It's in verses 1 and 2, "...that, if any (husbands) obey not the word, they also may without the word be won by the conversation of the wives. While they behold your chaste conversation coupled with fear."

The revelation I received may not be for everybody, but it might help you. While you are engaging in a conversation with your husband, he may not believe or agree with what you are saying. But, with a tenderness of heart, let a sweet tone project through your mouth. It will cause him to stop and listen to you without ever agreeing, and he'll be won. For certain, he doesn't understand the Word of God or your relationship with God. However, he understands your loving, modest, and pure mannerism. And your attitude will change him.

I began to practice and disclose this finding to other women. I share with them that respect and love will change their husbands whether they are saved or not saved.

It worked for me. Even though Herb was saved, there was some fine-tuning considered necessary in his belief system. He gave ear to me because I was adorned with integrity, honesty, and respect. My outlook changed. I was happy being home with him on Saturdays, cuddled in bed under his arms. Shopping didn't cease; it just wasn't done as often with my friends. But it increased with him.

Adorn yourself, and prepare your heart for his entrance. Fall at his feet when he approaches the doorway of your heart. Light up his path with your tenderness.

WORSHIP HIM IN SPIRIT AND IN TRUTH

In our ministry, we also encourage men and women to have intimacy with God. We want them to develop closeness with Him because of their love. Married couples have changed. They apply obedience in their daily activities.

In women's personal Bible study, women are asked to explain how they worship God. Some concluded with, "I bow down," "I lie prostrate on the floor," or "I sit on the floor or sit in a chair and bow my head for worship."

The way in which they choose to worship is physical. Getting in position is the essence of worship. Some stated, "Before worship, we cleanse our bodies and anoint with oil." Either way is an act of faith because "it pleases God" (Hebrews 11:6).

Worship is a devotion or admiration shown towards Christ. God is looking for "true worshippers" (John 4:24). Further in the book of John, chapter 11 tells a story about Jesus' friendship with Mary and Martha, sisters of Lazarus.

Lazarus died, and Martha heard that Jesus was coming to town. She went to meet Him, but Mary stayed at the house. Martha saw the Lord and with an attitude said to Him, "Lord, if You had been here, my brother would not have died."

Jesus said to her, "Your brother will rise again"

Martha said to him, "I know that he will rise again in the resurrection at the last day."

Jesus said unto her, "I am the resurrection and the life: He who believes in Me, though he may die, he shall live. And whoever lives and believes in Me shall never die. Do you believe this?"

She said to him, "Yes, Lord, I believe that You are the Christ, the Son of God, who is to come into the world." And when she had said these things, she went her way and secretly called Mary her sister, saying, "The Master is come, and calls for you" (John 11:20-28 NKJV).

Although Christ heard Martha, He wanted a worshipper. Therefore, He called for Mary. A true worshipper doesn't have to pray before answering the call; he or she has already prayed and is ready to move.

Mary got up quickly and went to him. Jesus had not entered the village. In fact, He was where Martha left him. Before Mary got to where Jesus was, several things happened. First, the Jews who were with her observed how quickly she moved, and they got up to follow her, thinking that she was going to the grave to weep.

She moved quickly to be with the Lord. It wasn't a second thought; she moved because of His call and her love for Him. Too often, we don't follow Christ immediately because we have to think about it, pray, and then speak in other tongues before we move.

Mary met with Jesus, and she didn't speak a word. She fell at his feet and worshipped him. Then, she spoke gently, "Lord, if You had been here, my brother would not have died."

Jesus was touched and moved by her tears, and saw how the Jews were weeping. He asked, "Where have you laid him?"

They said to Him, "Lord, come and see."

And some of them said, "Could not this Man, who opened the eyes of the blind, also have kept this man from dying?"

Then Jesus, again groaning in Himself, came to the tomb. It was a cave, and a stone lay against it. Jesus said, "Take away the stone" (John 11:32-39 NKJV).

Then they took away the stone from the place where the dead man was lying. And Jesus lifted up *His* eyes and said, "Father, I thank You that You have heard Me. And I know that You always hear Me, but because of the people who are standing by I said this, that they may believe that You sent Me." Now when He had said these things, He cried with a loud voice, "Lazarus, come forth." And he who had died came out bound hand and foot with grave clothes, and his face was wrapped with a cloth. Jesus said to them, "Loose him, and let him go" (John 11:41-44 NKJV).

Jesus wants to resurrect men and women from a dead situation, to make them become worshippers, and then, to have them worship Him in spirit and in truth. Are you one of those people? Are you ready to be resurrected from the dead issues that you can't clearly remember but that you keep clutched in the palm of your hand? God wants you to die from dead issues, and live again in Him. Give God permission to resurrect some things in your life.

A RESURRECTION ACT OF THANKSGIVING

In the following chapter, six days before the Passover Jesus came to Bethany, where Lazarus lived who was now raised from the dead. I believe that as a resurrection act of thanksgiving, a meal was prepared for Him which Martha served. To communicate thanksgiving, "Mary took a pound of ointment of spikenard, very costly, and anointed the feet of Jesus. She wiped his feet with her hair, and the house was filled with the odour of the ointment" (John 12:3KJV).

Then said one of His disciples, Judas Iscariot, Simon's son, which should betray him, "Why was not his ointment sold for three hundred pence, and given to the poor?" This he said not that he cared for the poor; but because he was a thief, and had the bag, and bare what was put therein. Then said Jesus, "Let her alone: against the day of my burying has she kept this. For the poor always ye have with you: but me ye have not always" (John 12:4-8).

The element of the story in John eleven that we didn't get was how Jesus rebuked Martha for complaining. Yet, some time later, Mary asked the same question and was not rebuked. What made the difference? Her approach was different.

Martha saw him and began complaining. Mary, however, reached the location where Jesus was and bowed at His feet to worship Him. Then she spoke, "Lord, if You had been here, my brother would not have died."

As she asked the identical question, tears fell from her eyes, and He was touched by her emotion. The key message for us all is that she knew what He loved. Remember previously, she anointed His head and sat at His feet. She worshipped Him in spirit and in truth. Jesus declares that He is seeking for such to worship Him in spirit and in truth (John 4:24).

We must get in that place where Mary was. You have the right to ask questions. But your heart must be true. Mary's heart was right. She was in right standing with Christ. She worshipped Him before asking the straightforward question.

You must worship your husband, the lord of your life. Cry a little. Show your emotions, and receive from him. I know you don't show emotion easily. You don't cry, either. You weren't born that way. Listen to me closely. Jesus wept, and that same tenderness is in us.

To get what you want, why can't you share a few tears? If tears moved Christ, you must believe that tears will move your husband. I'm not speaking of making tears like in the movies, where an onion forces tears. Real, genuine tears move him. Use wisdom! Come down out of the high chair, and be real. This is a real problem with a real solution. The answer is before you. Are you going to accept it? What are you going to do?

Being stubborn is not the cure. To make it real, rebellion can be a killer to your soul. That is not the solution, "For rebellion is as the sin of witchcraft, and stubbornness is as iniquity and idolatry (1 Samuel 15:23).

Submit to the word of the Lord. He instructs us to humble ourselves before our mates. Don't reject the Lord. He will surely reject you (1 Samuel 15:23). As you worship the Lord in spirit and in truth, His love will flow in you.

As you worship your husband, you will steal his heart. Your lips, from a previous kiss, are like sweetness of the honeycomb. This is how Solomon puts it in Song of Solomon 4:9-12, 15 (NIV).

"You have stolen my heart, my sister, my bride; you have stolen my heart with one glance of your eyes, with one jewel of your necklace. How delightful is your love, my sister, my bride! How much more pleasing is your love than wine, and the fragrance of your perfume than any spice! Your lips drop sweetness as the honeycomb, my bride; milk and honey are under your tongue. The fragrance of your garments is like that of Lebanon. You are a garden locked up, my sister, my bride; you are a spring enclosed, a sealed fountain. You are a garden fountain, a well of flowing water streaming down from Lebanon."

Steal his heart, my sister. Massage his face with the softness of your hands, and gently touch your lips on his lips so that your radiant heat melts his heart to seduce you.

HIS LOVE IS BETTER THAN WINE

There are times when men don't get the honor they deserve from women. They want a private moment with their wives. He doesn't want children with running noses. Just with you he wants to be. Although you love each other, you have conflicting schedules for intimacy.

When time is available, you are too tired. He tries to be intimate, but you are slow in your response. He wants a kiss, but you are too exhausted. Take the time, and let him kiss you with the kisses of his mouth. His love is better than wine. Go into the bedroom with silk rose petals, shape them in a heart centered on the bed, and put chocolate covered strawberries at the mouth of the bed. Bundle up; lie all night against his chest. Light the fire in his heart with sweet fragrances of your favorite perfume, and tell him how pleasing his name is to you.

He is the king of your life, a pleasant sight in your presence. He is like a bouquet of flowers in the garden of your soul. He will squeeze you with his strong muscles in the tender manner in which he holds a fragile butterfly. He shall call you a beautiful woman, touching your cheeks and kissing your neck as he accents your neck with a long string of pearls. How beautiful you are, his beloved woman. Your eyes are soft like doves. Kiss him again and again, and take him into that sacred place with your heart and soul (Song of Solomon 1:1-17).

Marriage is an institution ordained by God. A woman is a gift given by God to man. Both are made for each other to love, admire, and adore their beauty (Genesis 12:26; Matthew 19:4-6). Marriage is sacred. It is designed by God for men and women to grow together in respect to enjoy every moment of their togetherness.

Marriage is not a means to an end. It is the beginning of righteousness in the hearts of couples who were perhaps looking for love in all the wrong places, but who found love in each other through the Spirit of God.

Together, they understand that the husband is the head of the wife and that the wife is subject to her husband. Some people know that marriage is for them; it's better for them to marry than to burn. I didn't quite understand the burn portion, but I knew from an early age that I should be married.

CHAPTER 10

When Men Cheat, Women Become Quiet

*G*od did not design marriage for man and woman to have control over one another, but for each of them to love with a tender heart.

EVERYTHING THEY NEED IS IN HIM.

It is appalling to hear, when a man wants to leave, that he leaves his relationship for boredom and old age. These two reasons cause men to give up on their marriages. It is even more shocking to hear that women leave their relationships to have better sex and generate more money with another man. What is happening in today's marriages?

God has everything we need. Why not turn to Him and not away from one another? He is power; we are power. He is joy; we are joy. He can do all things; through Him, we can do all things. Because we can do all things, strategize! Organize a plan to save your marriage. Woman, put on your boxing gloves in the Spirit, and get your man.

You must have joy, not sorrow, as you go into the enemy's camp to take your husband back.

There may be another woman in his life, but you are his wife. For some unknown reason, he is committing adultery; but you vowed to love, support, and promote him in sickness and in health. A sickness came on him, and you can get to the root of it, to heal and nurture him back to health. None of us like the fact that our husbands are lurking after another woman when they have us.

What do we do when he wants to leave? If he is not saved, let him go. That's scriptural! It's difficult to understand why he wants to leave. It's hard to let go of the man you love. No matter what the outcome, the hurt is still there from those cruel words: "I'm leaving." When he changes his mind, in your head you think, "What happened that he changed his mind?" If truth be told, that's not the real issue. The real issue is whether you are willing to forgive and be faithful to him.

If he is talking to hear himself chatter, making redundant threats, but not making provision to leave home, then get on your knees, fast, and pray. Moreover, romance him back to health and life.

Some wives look for a new relationship to find happiness. Happiness is in each of us. We must let it come forth. We don't have to leave home to get satisfaction. It is in us. It takes time and effort to get it out. Then, we don't have to uncover that which we feel is missing. Again, what we need is inside our consciences, hearts, and minds.

We are the Lord's little children, and we should not want for anything. Psalm 23:1 tells us that the Lord is our shepherd and we shall not want. Psalm 24:1 states, "the earth is the Lord's, and all its fullness, the world and those who dwell therein." The earth will give back to us that which we cry out. Cry out for your husband's healing.

DRIFTING AWAY LIKE THE WAVES

My first marriage was disastrous forty-three years ago. I thought we were one unit, our souls knitted, but I felt a shifting in my spirit. He became irresponsible and with that, lies were spoken with confidence. At times, I was confident that I was making everything up.

He was not taking care of the home. The rent was behind, and we were near eviction. I wanted to leave him, but there was such an undeniable connection between him and the children. I didn't want to break that off, and I didn't have to worry long. He hid from the landlord, but eventually the landlord chased him down and told him that we had to move. Our relationship was drifting away like the waves in the ocean.

PUT IT AT THE FRONT DOOR

Prior to us moving, Lloyd came home from work one evening with an attitude: fussing about nothing and stirring up a physical fight. Evidently, the other woman made him angry, and he wanted to take it out on me. Previously during the day, the Lord prepared me for the great event, but I ignored His voice. He spoke this to me: "Break the mop in half and place the handle at the front door for your protection."

I couldn't conceive in my heart that this message came from God. It had me wanting to hurt him, and that mop was my only protection. I threw the entire mop in the field across from the house and continued with my housework. A few hours later the Lord spoke again, "I told you to get the mop and break it in half. He is coming home to fight you. Go and get it and put it at the front door."

The force of that voice was so real that I knew it was the Lord speaking to me. So I did it!

Later that evening, Lloyd came into the apartment argumentative, complaining, and pushing me around. I told him that I didn't want to fight. But he continued pushing me roughly. The force from the push knocked me so hard that I fell over the gold swing-back chair that my mother gave us as a wedding gift. Without delay, the fall made me see stars.

I crawled backward on my hands and feet, trying to get out of his way, and while moving I felt the handle of the stick. I gripped it in my hand, and at that instant a blissful feeling crossed the threshold of my mind: "Destroy him." I knew the fight was on and there was nothing I could do except defend and protect myself. As he came towards me, I swung and hit him, knocking him backward. I was able to rise above my circumstance, and I swung and hit him over and over until I was exhausted. As I hit him, I was yelling and screaming. I suppose my voice carried to the next door neighbor's house, where my grandmother's former church member lived. She called my mother and told her, "Come quickly. Your daughter is screaming, and it sounds serious."

My mother and eldest brother Walter rushed quickly to the house. As they walked in, Lloyd stretched out a bruised arm and said, "She is crazy; look what she did to me." He was attempting to shift the blame from himself to me. My family knew me, and they knew that I would never start a fight or pass the first blow.

My three oldest brothers taught me the art of protecting myself through wrestling, kick boxing, and fist fighting. I was well-rounded in defending myself. I just didn't like to fight. I thought it was an ignorant way of dealing with problems.

My mother sat us down and communicated that we should live godly before our children, that we must talk and not fight. As for me, I wanted out of the marriage. I felt that if he hit me once, he would do it twice. I was not his punching bag or his sparring partner. He wasn't Muhammad Ali, and I wasn't Sonny Liston.

That night, I left with the children. I didn't go back to the apartment. We were being evicted, and I could not conceptualize that God wanted me to live in an abusive environment. I had not seen that before, and I wasn't going to take his hitting me and sleeping with another woman. I couldn't control him sleeping with her, but I could make a statement that would take me and my children out of harm's way.

SHE SHOT HIM DOWN

For what I am about to speak, I apologize to all the grandmothers of today who want their granddaughters to encounter the same type of happiness they did. You should want the best for your grandchildren. It is important that they grow up and that a special man finds them and then marries them. But nowadays, men and women view life differently. They want to give possession [control] before marriage. He wants to shack up, and she allows it. She wants him to hit her; somehow she feels it will prove his love. That's revolting! So is a man who feels that it is permissible for his woman to hit him, striking him from cheek to cheek on a continuous basis. That behavior is also revolting.

The little girl in me that grew up with grandmother's thoughts matured early and wanted the assurance that her man would love her, honor her, and treat her with respect.

Subsequent to leaving my husband, I thought about our getting back together for the children's sake. I knew they'd be taken care of, but who was going to take care of me? Lloyd used to have vision for the family, but it became difficult for me to follow him after he abandoned the vision. He gave his word to work to provide for his family. But he broke every promise by not working, by or taking days off to be with another woman whose aim was to separate his family.

He drank and got drunk on beer and wine. But I drank the new wine that represented life and got drunk in the Spirit. We didn't agree on too much of anything. I was willing to submit, but he failed by having the affair and by wanting to fight me. He released me, and I left!

I disappointed my grandmother, but I couldn't take the abuse. I loved her and believed in what she wanted for me, but Lloyd wasn't my knight in shining armor.

The other woman succeeded, and we drifted away. Our goals changed. Late one summer evening in 1966, I received a telephone call asking me to come to the local medical center. Lloyd was brought in for a gun shot wound to the stomach. Months before, I had told him to be careful. I saw him shot, and I saw a woman stepping over him, running across the street to an upstairs apartment. He was leaving from visiting with his children. He stopped at my mother's gate and said, "You are jealous. She loves me. She will never do that." Sure enough, the other woman shot him.

I went to see him while he recovered in the hospital from the gun shot to his stomach. When I walked in the room, an elderly woman was chatting with him. I nodded my head and took a seat. She was a stranger. I didn't know her, and she surely didn't know me. I heard her say, "Lloyd, you should get a divorce from your wife and marry my sister. Y'all should get saved and live a good life." She looked at me and asked, "Are you related to him?"

My response was "Yes."

She further asked, "Are you his sister?"

"No," I replied.

"Are you his niece?"

I stated, "No."

She persisted with her last question, "Are you his cousin?"

I looked directly at her like she was a silly woman, and with a smile on my face I replied, "I am his wife."

The woman almost choked, trying to get out of her mouth these words, "I'm sorry."

I stated, "No offense. They ought to be together. He should divorce me and marry your sister."

The woman believed in the sanctity of marriage. She could care less about my children. She wanted her sister married so that she didn't have to be an adulterous woman. She was shaken that I agreed with her. She saw them married, and I saw us separated. There was no way for me to take him back. Even if I wanted to reunite, I didn't need to watch over my back for the rest of my life, wondering if it was safe to leave my house for fear of her shooting me or my children. My family didn't need the drama.

Even though Lloyd and I separated, we promised to keep the door of communication open. But he reneged on his promise and shut the door. Our wedding vows were real, and they needed to be protected. Yet in our circumstance, we aborted the plan of God. Vows are not to be broken easily, nor should they be taken likely. Wedding vows are made unto death. It is better not to vow than to vow and not pay (Ecclesiastes 5:5).

OUR LOVE IS TOO IMPORTANT

Marriage was the ultimate goal to fulfill and bring to a climax what God intended marriage to be: healthy, blessed, and great. Men and women are obligated to build a relationship of togetherness.

Women were chosen to be the man's hope, ray of sunshine, and most importantly, his good thing. As his good thing, we have something that the other woman doesn't have, and that is the heart of our man. We have that extra something that the other woman doesn't have.

As I grew older and matured in Christ, in my second marriage I can say, "So what if he cheated. He made a terrible mistake." Come on, ladies; get him back! Forgive him, and fix yourself up. Wear expensive perfume and sexy clothes, and massage his lips with long kisses. This may appear to be hard at first, but surrender to humility and give up the stubborn, false determination of wanting to let go when you know that you don't. He can be won.

Dismiss what those friends have told you. "Girl, if I were you, I would make him compensate for what he did." No they wouldn't. They are in a more desperate situation than you. They are battered physically; you are battered verbally. I'm not suggesting that men should batter women. I'm saying change your words, and they will change him. You know what it takes to draw your man close to you. Do it!

Rudeness can make us do stupid things. At the onset of my marriage with Herb, I didn't feel he was husband material. Also, I wasn't prepared to be his wife. He had an overwhelming responsible of a new wife with three children. At times he was discombobulated as he organized our new life. His smile and the softness of his voice were great. From a spiritual perspective, when women saw him they would see the enormous baggage and turn away: there was no beauty that they should desire him (Isaiah 53:2).

At last my waiting would pay off. I had a man who needed me. I had a man that women would not seek. I was wrong. They looked beyond his obligations and went after his anointing. What should have caught my attention was when we were both working at the college. One of the counselors came to my office, which was located in a very small area away from anybody of importance. She came to tell me, "Herbert and I were in a meeting, and he told me, 'Never wear those old grey shoes. You are looking good from your head to your legs, but those shoes got to go.'"

She backed up against the wall and came out with a loud chuckle. I thought she was too old to act like a young school girl with her first compliment. She wasn't important enough to me even to talk with him about the incident. But that was the first sign of attraction.

That should have told me that other women would be looking at him. After we were married, he told me of an incident with one of his colleagues. When they went on an assignment for the college, the first night, this woman came to his room, knocked on the door, and stated frantically, "A man was at my door and I was frightened." Why not a call to security, then him? That was a plot. How silly she was to run from a secure environment to an unsecured environment |through the hall| in sexy red pajamas. Months after they returned, he was fired. She was his director. He was fired because he failed to provide her with that special protection.

We were a great couple, but I wasn't all that great of a wife. Plus, I was rude in my prayer life, and my search for spiritual worth made me forget to seek daily after my husband. At the age of fifty, my husband fell to the desire of a younger woman. I was devastated. And that staggered me back to reality.

At one point, pride told me to walk away. My heart told me to stay and fight. I could have given up, but I didn't. I thought to myself, "Our love is too important for me to give up." I fought for my man.

In prayer, the Lord revealed to me who she was, and I began to pray for her deliverance. My prayer was for a single man who was in ministry to find her. It was obvious that she was interested in ministers; my prayers were deliberately directed in this manner. I figured she needed a minister to call her own. My husband did not belong to her. She stopped wanting my husband. She left my anointed husband alone. Her minister found her, and she married her man. It didn't matter how many times she had written her first name to go with his last name; she was not going to have my husband.

The marriage you have doesn't have to be worse than it actually is. Sometime later, Herb told me that he wanted me to ask him to leave. The devil was a liar! We are both saved; I couldn't do that. For me to do that would have meant that I had fallen to the trickery of the enemy. Not so, I put on my war clothes. I put on the whole armor of God to stand against the wiles of the devil.

"We were not wrestling against flesh and blood, but against principalities; powers, rulers of darkness of this world, and against spiritual wickedness in high places" (Ephesians 6:11-12).

You are not fighting against flesh and blood, but you are in warfare. The weapons of our warfare are not carnal, but mighty through God (2 Corinthians 10:4). The words were addressed to the apostles, and we do not find that they carried swords as they pursued ministry [marriage]. Can we assume that when the Lord said, "Put up thy sword," He meant that we should put away any thought or plan of fighting against men to concentrate on Him as we participate in spiritual warfare?

THE LUXURY IS GREATER THAN THE AFFAIR

There is no greater reward for marriage than giving ourselves to our mates. Our giving should be cheerful and generous. Herb and I have been married for twenty-five years. I am glad we took a stand and withstood in the evil days. With my lions girt with truth and having on the breastplate of righteousness (Ephesians 6:13, 14), we eventually stood together to defeat the devil.

I still enjoy the luxury of telephone calls, flowers, and hearing the softness of his voice as he tells me how great and special I am. Even when he doesn't tell me these things, the softness of his voice excites my spirit and makes me humble before him.

It is a gratification being married to Herb. Every morning he calls me his beautiful woman. In the past, he has called me a nagging woman. Now he even says to me, "Sam, you are a good woman."

Even when we were angry at each other and didn't speak, I knew in his heart he had a special relationship with my heart, mind, and spirit.

Certainly, we have aggravated one another since that ordeal by either an act or spoken words. Yes, we have been on the wrong page, and you may be thinking that we gave the enemy room for entrance. We did, but we overcame. We felt that our love was so mighty that it would overcome any obstacles placed in our path.

God gave us a test, and we won! The devil is mad. But we over-came all those obstacles.

If we overcame challenges and survived, you can come together with your husband and treat him with the honor he deserves. Men, you can love your wives as Christ loves the church. Both of you can communicate effectively by your standards, not by the standards of someone who is lonely, who has never been married, who has a difficult time getting a man, or who is incapable of keeping one.

Your husband cheated on you, but you can get even by being quiet. 1 Thessalonians 3:11 teaches us to, "Study to be quiet, and do your own business, and work with your own hands." The Message Bible says it in this manner: "May God our Father himself and our Master Jesus clear the road to you!" (1 Thessalonians 3:11) Speak God's Word on your situation. Your husband will return home in peace. But you must put it in action that every time he leaves home, he comes back in peace with a heart of thanksgiving. Time is of the essence, and it's precious. You have assurance from God. Work the Word; the Word will work for you.

CHEATING DOES WHAT CHEATING DOES

God has not called us to live as fornicators or adulterers, but to live a life of holiness (1 Thessalonians 4:7). He is the Lord your God; you shall sanctify yourselves and be holy, "for I am holy" says the Lord in Leviticus 11:44.

Cheaters do what cheaters do. They make promises, and at will rescind. Cheating is similar to sinning. Prophetess A. R. Maxwell told me once, "There is no need to be upset with sinners. They do what they know, and that is to sin."

We have also made a promise to love God always, and we deserted prayer to vacation with friends. On vacation, prayer is usually avoided. Our prayer time is still reserved for Him. Wrong, Wrong, Wrong!

What else have we done to God? Cheating does what cheating does. Our daily living and commitment to Him has not been great.

We lied, and He forgave us. We stole, and He gave us another opportunity to get it right with Him and with man.

Now is the time to make good choices for our marriages. We can make good choices that will bring abundance, or we can make bad decisions that will bring defeat, hardship, and unnecessary struggles. The devil would like very much to destroy your marriage, but don't let him.

Fight back. Brush off defeat, and put on offense. You can't continue to sit back saying, "I'll let him go." Why let him? If we are going to reach our husbands, we need to know something about where they are going. Possess the land. In prayer, spy out the land to take charge. Even as the children of Israel sent the twelve men to "spy out the land," we need to kneel in prayer to find out about the other woman. Is she strong or weak? Is she pleasant or harsh to him? Is she young or old? It is not a question whether he will return home. The answer is that he shall return.

Quietly, you have to find out what drew him to her. What emotional needs is she meeting? Don't hurry to challenge her or become her competition. You need ammunition. Use wisdom to gather information. When there is no information to gather, work with what you have. Your man is the only reference point. Leave the rest alone.

As God instructed Moses to send out twelve men from each tribe to scout out the land, Moses did. So they went up and explored the land from the wilderness of Zin as far as Rehob, near Lebo-hamath. Going northward, they passed first through the Negev and arrived at Hebron, where Ahiman, Sheshai, and Talmai—all descendants of Anak—lived. When they came to what is now known as the valley of Eshcol, they cut down a cluster of grapes so large that it took two of them to carry it on a pole between them! They also took samples of pomegranates and figs. At that time, the Israelites renamed the valley Eshcol—"cluster"—because of the cluster of grapes they had cut there (Numbers 13:21-24).

THE SCOUTING REPORT

After exploring the land for forty days, the men returned to Moses, Aaron, and the people of Israel at Kadesh in the wilderness of Paran. They reported to the whole community what they had seen and showed them the fruit they had taken from the land. This was their report to Moses: "We arrived in the land you sent us to see, and it is indeed a magnificent country—a land flowing with milk and honey. Here is some of its fruit as proof. But the people living there are powerful, and their cities and towns are fortified and very large. We also saw the descendants of Anak who are living there! The Amalekites live in the Negev, and the Hittites, Jebusites, and Amorites live in the hill country. The Canaanites live along the coast of the Mediterranean Sea and along the Jordan Valley" (Numbers 13:25-29).

But Caleb tried to encourage the people as they stood before Moses. "Let's go at once to take the land," he said. "We can certainly conquer it!"

But the other men who had explored the land with him answered, "We can't go up against them! They are stronger than we are!" So they spread discouraging reports about the land among the Israelites: "The land we explored will swallow up any who go to live there. All the people we saw were huge. We even saw giants there, the descendants of Anak. We felt like grasshoppers next to them, and that's what we looked like to them!" (Numbers 13:30-33). Even though the report was overwhelming for them to fathom, Caleb believed that they could possess the land. This must be your feeling. It doesn't matter how long he has been seeing her; you can possess the land through prayer and patience. Look back on how you began your marriage. God has blessed your efforts even though some lacked accurate planning. Optimistically, after your experiences, you will have the ability to help save other marriages throughout the nation.

YOU ARE UNIQUE

This is a difficult statement for me to make. Again I don't mean to harm or offend anyone. But some women think, "I can't take him back. It's hard to forgive him. She can do that because she is an older woman."

Not so, it was done because we who are mature didn't want to end our marriages and not see the salvation of the Lord move in our lives. Some women can't stay in a relationship; they give up while they are stuck on stupid and parked on dumb.

You are unique, and you will not let pride destroy your marriage. You don't have to tolerate the mess, but you can survive the marriage. Pride has allowed women to let their men go. The fear of what people say will not help you. Let them say whatever, and you get back with your man.

Some will call you a fool. Be a fool with wisdom who went into the enemy camp to get her man back. Get over people, and go to the next plateau in God. Be happy, not sad! Don't think about what people say; hear God's voice.

YOU ARE NOT A FOOL

There are some people from whom you should never take advice. People who are lonely and alone are dangerous when giving advice. For the most part, they feel they should be with a man or have a husband. Check out their behavior! You know them. You see them every day. You include them in your family issues because they are your friends. When they see your face, they are sympathetic. Yet behind your back, they tell another friend, "I don't see how she takes that from him. She is a fool."

Wrong. You are not the fool; she is for repeating what you told her in confidence. That strong-willed, self-centered, arrogant, lacking purpose woman broke a vow to pray and comfort you.

In all honesty, you desire to have a friend, but you don't have a general faithful friend to whom you can open your heart. Your friends will broadcast your husband's infidelity, only to hide what is really happening in their dysfunctional marriages. For public appearance they are together. But they are separated, sleeping with multiple partners while conducting Christian counseling seminars on marriage and the family. The devil is a liar and the father of it (John

8:44). A fool is not what you need to call a friend. "A fool's mouth is his [her] destruction" (Proverbs 18:7a). But a friend is someone who will stick closer than a brother (Proverbs 18:24). "The words of a talebearer are as wounds, and they go down into the innermost parts of the belly" (Proverbs 18:8). Covenant vows were broken between a man and his wife. One specific woman was devastated to find that her friend, whom she took in confidence, snared her husband's name throughout the city. She came to me for counseling. She was a dear family member, seeking advice concerning the broken covenant.

She wasn't certain if he was having an affair, but she observed a behavioral change. He used to have conversations with her and listen, but now he was constantly daydreaming, not hearing her words. When visitors came to the house, he would go into the bedroom and not come out until they were gone. He gave permission for them to come, and this is how he treated them. She was embarrassed of his rudeness, but she dealt fervently with his attitude.

In her heart she knew another woman was in his life. She asked him, but he denied that he was having an affair. The most crucial thing she did was pray. Her prayer was for God to reveal his behavior and whether he was having an affair.

During the hurricane season in September 1994, there was a terrible storm. The rain beat down hard on the windshield. The wiper blades didn't appear to do their job, but she drove slowly through the streets, trying to make it home as limbs off trees fell in front of her. She barely made it home.

When she arrived, he wasn't home. Her heart was pounding, longing for him, wondering where he was. Her spirit was suspicious that he might be in an accident. Be careful of what you think and ask; it will materialize. She fell on her knees to pray; in her spirit she saw where he was, in the safekeeping of a woman's arms.

She said, "Prophetess, I was furious when I saw him with that woman. But I was more interested in his safety than anything else. It was late when he got home, and I didn't mention anything about what the Lord revealed. I was happy to see him safe and home. Yet in the back of my mind, the woman was there." She further stated, "I wanted to do something, but I didn't know what." Some of you are saying, "She was really foolish. That couldn't be me. Is she really that naïve?"

I know you'd have confronted the other woman. You would have gone to her house or job asking her to leave your husband alone. Most likely you would have gone to the house and given her a beat-down. Trust me, knowing this woman, she would have if God hadn't prevented her from acting unseemly. Believe me, this family member was qualified to behave like a brawler. Her brothers taught her to defend herself, and she wasn't scared. She'd tackle the biggest and the boldest when approached with stupid matters. But that behavior would have brought reproach to her husband.

Her desire was for him to see that she was a chaste woman who held him in high esteem. And too, she had no business going to the other woman's house, and her husband should have never gone there, either. She concluded, "For the first time in a long time, I wanted to reach back into my ghetto days to stomp her butt, and not like Kirk Franklin's song. *'And all the people say: stomp.'* I wanted to put a beat-down on her. But I also knew that this was a test. I had to conquer this test to go to the next level in Christ. I was recently called into ministry when this affair occurred. My husband's desires brought mistrust into our marriage. Because I was a praying woman, I knew that God was going to take care of this problem. In my heart I knew that God was going to repay him. Also, our prayers could be hindered (1 Peter 3:7-12) for his selfishness."

As months went by, the other woman was driven away from her husband. "As smoke is driven away, so drive them away: as wax melteth before the fire, so let the wicked perish at the presence of God" (Psalm 68:2). She said, "I knew if the other woman didn't let him go and repent, she'd melt before the fire. She touched my husband, and because I'm anointed, a part of me was snatched out of his heart. She had to disappear."

Shortly after our talk, they called seeking counseling. The other woman called the couple's house early one morning to speak with the husband. But his wife answered. The other woman was desperate. She had a son, and she began to say that it was this man's child. When that didn't work, she told of the jewelry and the car he bought her. Finally, after having enough of the madness, his wife stated, "You have all that, but you don't have what you want: my man. I still have him."

Before his wife, the husband confessed his sin and struggles, seeking support with his addictions. He wasn't too thrilled about coming to me, but he yielded his pride and came. To a man, any type of counseling is difficult.

In the course of the counseling, both repented. Gently I spoke, "Let it die! You are praying and you have put the Word on the situation. You are on the road of recovery. You should no longer be afraid or fearful. From Psalm 27:1-2 you know that 'the LORD is your light and your salvation; whom shall you fear? The LORD is the strength of your life; of whom shall you be afraid? When the wicked, even your enemies and your foes, came upon you to eat up your flesh, they stumbled and fell.'"

CHECK YOURSELF BEFORE YOU WRECK YOURSELF

As you enter counseling, never bring revenge to the counseling table. That will heat things up, not solve anything. This will not restore marriage; it will persist to annihilate what you are attempting to build.

With the right disposition, marriage can be healthy again. The devil uses sinners to push Christians around, and we are not supposed to speak for ourselves. They think that we should not guard our hearts and that we should let them do to us what they will. Again, the devil is a liar!

Even as the weaker vessels, women are not stupid. Yet sinners want to push us to the limit. When that happens, what do you do about your emotions? When your emotions get the best of you, cry. When a woman cries, she thinks. Think twice, my sister, prior to speaking.

In fact, you need to check yourself before you wreck yourself. There is no need to deflate the relationship with the other woman. That issue had to be dealt with, not with her, the third party, but with you and your husband. Yet, she can not be brushed under the rug out of sight, and dismissed as if she never existed.

He cheated, but the beauty is that you are still longing for him. Why is this? You are longing for your knight in shining armor.

You were blamed for his inconsiderate manner, and many fought you for the downfall in the marriage. You were also charged for his unkindness, his criticism, and his sarcastic tongue. What did you do with that abuse? You kept your tongue and loved him. You honored him and put the Word of God on your marriage.

The Spirit of God drove the other woman away. Consider this, for revelation. Just as smoke is driven away, his thoughts were driven away from her and brought back to you; as wax melts before the fire, so let the wicked words [her thoughts of separation] perish at the presence of God (Psalm 68:2).

WHAT ARE YOU GOING TO DO?

Philippians 2:4 tells us to look not every man on his own things, but every man also on the things of others. Forget about your feelings, and offer a helping hand.

The hands of the husband who tinkered with his marriage can't afford to do anything except to offer a hand to be sorrowful for his actions and to ask for forgiveness. Although he wasn't caught in the act of adultery, his wife found out after the fact. It's time for him to give up pride and arrogance and get his woman's trust back. He should confess his wrong and admit that he needs his wife. He needs her hand to assist him. Calling her nasty names, telling her that she is fat as a cow and lazy is not going to cut it. Critical sarcasm in front of her friends is no longer amusing. They don't see the humor. Husband, you were caught; what are you going to do? She doesn't need to do anything except remain the same. This is your time to demonstrate faithfulness.

A woman who's in love will go the last mile. But when she sees that her husband is not willing to change and when she exceeds her limit of understanding, nobody will be able to change her mind.

You heard the expression that hell will freeze over. Well, that's how it will be. My brother, there is nothing you can do to get her to change her mind. She can be in pain, but she will refuse to give in.

The majority of the time, it will take God, not a minister, a friend, or a family member to change her mind. It then becomes a God problem.

No matter what a man does in effort to make up for a wrong that has been done to her, his tender words will not renew her mind. He can't come at her in the old way with laughter, stating "Baby, you know I didn't mean that. Kiss your honey. Please forgive me." Go to the next level. That isn't working.

Take this from a woman who knows; I have been there and done that. It won't work without a clean heart and a renewed spirit. You can't go half the distance to that woman. Clean up your act and get it right.

As long as a woman has a good heart, she will forgive and forget a lot of things. I recommend that you "count it all joy when you fall into various trials" (James 1:2). "Cast all your cares on the Lord" (1 Peter 5:7). "Cast your burden on the Lord; He shall sustain you and will never permit the righteous to be moved" (Psalm 55:22). "Cast your bread upon the waters, for in many days it shall return" (Ecclesiastes 11:1). "Weeping may endure for a night but joy comes in the morning" (Psalm 30:5).

However, if your wife gets full of foolishness, your chances for forgiveness are slack. She can take her burdens to the Lord on Sunday in the AM service and pick them back up on Wednesday night in Bible Study. From her standpoint, you will suffer from the last time she remembers until your apology is felt in her spirit. Until that time, you will hear her voice.

The only reason you would not hear her voice, is if you packed your bags and took a rest from the environment. No, my brother, don't do that. You will demonstrate guilt. Your only interest should be to comfort that woman. This is not the time to be distant from the situation that you created. Clean up your act. Buy her good gifts, and apologize for the cruelty you brought into her life. Men, are you hearing this? Your wife is tired of the lies and deception. You messed up, but she is willing to help you clean up your mess.

To some women, this concept is ridiculous. "He messed up, but I have to help clean it up. I'm not the clean up woman." Move from non-productive thinking, and look at wisdom. It's better that you are the one to clean up, than to have that same woman clean up what you gave up after he messed up. This is great wisdom. Clap your hands for victory.

MARRIAGE IS NOT A GAME

Women who are full of anger and unforgiving want their husbands to stay in their hands so that they can dump them when feasible. Marriage is not a game. Don't go there. Evidently it is a woman's thing to keep a man in your hand, to want to control him, to have the urge to put your foot on top of him, to hold him in place.

Common sense tells you not to hold him down. Wisdom from God tells you to lift him up. When you hold him down, you keep yourself back. It's crazy, wanting to dominate someone, holding him in place. I don't know about you, but I don't want to stand still and not be productive. I want mobility to accomplish and reach goals, fulfilling what I believe are life's expectations for me to be successful. I don't have time to baby-sit, keeping watch over Herb.

Wisdom tells you to keep a watchful eye on your husband. After all, you are his helper. Help him to see what you see by phrasing things differently. Prepare your mind to speak the truth in wisdom by convincing him with your chaste manner that danger is ahead, lurking after him, trying to separate him from God.

Trusting in your marriage should be more important than how he made love to the other woman. What places he took her or whether he met her family is immaterial.

What is important? Did you tell him of the kiss and the pat on your rear end from another man with whom you weren't intimate? You had to feel wanted given that he was involved with someone else.

Now you say, "Don't go there." Why not? You went there. I know your situation was different; it was just an innocent little kiss and a gentle rub on your buttocks. Furthermore, he doesn't know, and what he doesn't know won't hurt him.

The same thing goes for you. What you didn't know almost destroyed your marriage. The things you suspected were unfounded;

you almost had a nervous breakdown. You don't want to confess, but he had to tell you everything he did.

Release him, and let the affair go. It's over. Forget the past, and move on. Stop insisting that he tell you how and when they were together. Trust me, you don't want to know the truth. You are not ready to handle that. Press forward! Place your mind on speed dial, and press on.

Paul states in Philippians 3:13-14 to forget those things which are behind and reach forward to those things which are ahead. Nine out of ten women have pressed toward the goal for the prize of the upward call of God in Christ Jesus. Now you press towards the goal and receive your prize.

CHAPTER 11

When the Woman Wants to Leave

*R*ecently, I was approached by one of the brothers in our ministry following Bible study. He asked, "What do you have planned for the men? We hurt, and we have pain. But everything is centered on women. We had a single's conference, but it was for women, not men."

Of course, my first words were, "You should speak with Bishop. Let him hear your concern. He can help you." For the first time in a very long time, I heard a young man saying that men are in great pain and that they need help with their pain. I felt saddened in my heart, but I couldn't adequately help the young man. The church committee felt that the subject matters already were for men and women. Each speaker elaborated on application, seeing you as a part of the solution, seeing you healed and out of bondage.

There aren't many men in our ministry. Bishop has been attempting to get the men together, but as usual, they're too busy. But now I know the truth. They are not too busy; they are simply afraid of showing emotion and articulating their issues in front of other men.

The young man was willing to speak with me in front of the crowd of women because he assumed we were no threat. He perhaps saw women as being the contributing factors for his misery. But a few days later, he was reluctant to have the same conversation with Bishop that he had with me. I mentioned what he said to Bishop, and he froze, hanging his head in shame. My thinking was that he would pick up where he left off talking with me. How could he get a release in his spirit, when he kept avoiding the opportunity to speak?

Most therapists and theologians feel that women are struggling with their identities. I beg to differ. I believe it is men who struggle with that problem. Women are praying, fasting, and discovering who they are.

The Constitution of the United States says that all men and women are created equal. In the sight of God, all men and women are created equal. Women can identify with their roles in comparison to the man. Women were created out of man (Genesis 2:21-25); they are man's glory (1 Corinthians 11:7-9). A woman is physically weaker than a man, but not necessarily spiritually weaker (1 Peter 3:7). She became subject to the man (Genesis 3:16).

These identities signify a woman's attributes. These things make her feel honorable and respectable. She knows that she is not limited to one particular area. She is meticulous, and she can do many things well.

In light of this, a woman will not leave her man unless doing so is crucial to her health or unless staying is detrimental to her children. Other than that, she will remain in the marriage if for no other reason than to prove the point that she does not have to be a divorce statistic.

In Genesis 3, observe that a woman was subject to her husband; yet, in 1 Samuel 25, see that a woman, Abigail, was stronger in a spiritual sense than her husband Nabal. She was beautiful and of a good understanding. Her husband, however, was rich, churlish, disrespectful, and evil.

When a woman wants to leave, she thinks her way out of leaving before she actually leaves. It is really hard for a woman to give up on her marriage. A man can clobber her, and she'll stay, hoping he will change. At times a woman's behavior will change to let you know that she is about to make a serious decision about her relationship. Women are like men; they have a desire to get out of a shaky relationship. They often choose to leave, seeking the joy and excitement of a new relationship, rather than deal with the issues. Even though a husband doesn't always understand a wife's behavioral change, she will not utter an explanation other than, "It's over, and I'm leaving." When at risk, she won't say a word. While her man is sleeping, she will leave with a note taped on the bedroom door, "See you later, not sooner."

A CRISIS SITUATION OF LIFE OR DEATH

In the case of Nabal and Abigail, the Bible doesn't tell us that she wanted to leave her evil husband. It suggests to the natural eye that she usurped authority over her husband. Perhaps so, but it was to save her life and her marriage.

Verse 5 tells how David sent ten young men to go to Nabal, who was shearing his sheep. It was harvest time, a moment for reaping and sharing. David said to the ten young men, "Go to Nabal, and greet him in my name. And say to him 'Peace *be* to you, peace to your house, and peace to all that you have! Now I have heard that you have shearers. Your shepherds were with us, and we did not hurt them, nor was there anything missing from them all the while they were in Carmel. Ask your young men, and they will tell you. Therefore let my young men find favor in your eyes, for we come on a feast day. Please give whatever comes to your hand to your servants and to your son David" (1 Samuel 25: 5-9 KJV). So when David's young men came, they spoke to Nabal according to all these words in the name of David, and waited.

David made this request because he had performed a valuable service for Nabal by serving as protection for his flocks in a time when Philistine raids were common. David performed a worthy, valuable service for Nabal, and then in harvest time he expected to be compensated.

In verses 10 through 12, Nabal replied negatively to David's request. He answered David's servants, and said, "Who is David, and who is the son of Jesse? There are many servants these days that break away every man from his master. Shall I then take my bread and my water and my slaughter that I have killed for my shearers, and give it to men whom I do not know?" So David's young men turned away, went, and told David Nabal's words.

David should have been proactive, but he reacted to Nabal's insult. David said to his men, "Gird [fasten] ye me every man his sword" (1 Samuel 25:13 KJV). So every man girded on his sword, and David also girded on his sword. And about four hundred men went with David, and two hundred stayed with the supplies. David was ready to fight. He was ready to destroy lives.

In the previous chapter, David spared Saul's life, but here he wanted to take Nabal's life. Whatever happened to 'turn the other cheek?' In Matthew 5:38-39 we see these words on retaliation. "You have heard that it hath been said, 'An eye for an eye, and a tooth for a tooth.' But I say unto you, that you resist not evil: but whosoever shall smite [hit] you on your right cheek, turn to the other also."

One of Nabal's servants witnessed his response to David's men and told Abigail. "Those men protected us and we lost nothing while they served as a wall for us, day and night. While we were in the field, we were not hurt. Now, we don't know what they will do. Nabal and his household will be harmed."

Abigail moved speedily. She knew that time was of importance and that something had to be done expeditiously. This wise woman took two hundred loaves of bread, two bottles of wine, five sheep already dressed, five measures of parched corn, a hundred clusters of raisins, and two hundred cakes of figs, and laid them on donkeys. And she said to her servants, "Go on before me; behold, I come after you" (1 Samuel 25:14-19).

She did not tell her husband of her decision, but she rode the donkey down the covert of the hill, and behold, David and his men came down against her; and she met them.

Now David had said, "Surely in vain I have protected all that this fellow has in the wilderness, so that nothing was missed of all that pertains to him. And he has repaid me evil for good. So and more also do God do unto the enemies of David, if I leave of all that pertain to him by the morning light" (verse 22).

David planned to kill Nabal and every male in his household. When Abigail saw David, she came down from her donkey, fell before him on her face, and bowed to the ground at his feet to speak.

"Upon me my lord, upon me let this iniquity be: and let your handmaid, I pray thee, speak in this audience, and hear the words of your handmaid. Let not my lord, I pray thee, regard this man of Belial, even Nabal is his name, and folly is with him: but I your handmaid saw not your young men of my lord, whom you sent. Now therefore, my lord, as the LORD lives, and as your soul lives, seeing the LORD has withholden you from coming to shed innocent blood, and from avenging yourself with your own hands, now let your enemies, and they that seek evil to my lord, be as Nabal. And now this gift your maidservant has brought to my lord, let it be given to the young men who follow my lord. I pray that you forgive the trespass of your handmaid. For the LORD will certainly make for my lord a sure house, because my lord fights the battles of the LORD, and evil is not found in you all your days. Yet a man is risen to pursue you and seek your soul, but the soul of my lord shall be protected in the bundle of the life with the LORD your God; and the souls of your enemies, them shall he sling out, as out of the middle of a sling. And it shall come to pass, when the LORD has done for my lord according to all the good that He has spoken concerning you, and shall have appointed you ruler over Israel; that this will be no grief to you, nor offense of heart to my lord, either that you shed blood causeless, or that my lord has avenged himself. But when the LORD has dealt well with my lord, then remember your handmaid." Then David said to Abigail "Blessed *is* the LORD God of Israel, who sent you this day to meet me! And blessed *is* your advice and blessed *are* you, because you have kept me this day from coming to bloodshed and from avenging myself with my own hand. For indeed, *as* the LORD God of Israel lives, which has kept me back from hurting you, except you had hastened and come to meet me, surely by morning light no males would have been left to Nabal." So David received from her hand that which she had brought him, and said to her, "Go up in peace to your house. See, I have listened to your advice and accepted [received] your person"

(1 Samuel 25:24-35).

HIS HEART WAS MERRY

Abigail went to Nabal, but he was having a feast in his house like the feast of a king. His behavior demonstrated that he wasn't respectful of his wife. He was having a feast, and she knew nothing of it. How could a man have a feast and not know that his wife wasn't in the house? At that time, a man's wife didn't participate in those events, but he should have known where she was. Besides that, she should have asked permission to see David, even though time was a factor and she didn't want to hear "No, you can't go." Because timing was crucial, she thought she did the right thing, but she left to see David without permission.

Nabal's heart was merry, and Abigail decided to tell him of the good news the next morning when he wasn't drunk anymore. As we look closer at this event, on the next morning when the wine was out of Nabal, she told him those things, and he lost all confidence. His heart died within. He had a heart attack or a stroke. The good news that David wasn't going to harm him may have caused his heart to fail. Or his anger at finding that Abigail took a portion of his possession and gave it to David could have been a cause.

Nabal chose to protect what was his and not to share with the man who previously protected him. He had a feast, and that behavior signified that his success was all about him and nobody else.

When a woman wants to leave, she will turn on you with words. There doesn't have to be another man for her to leave. Abigail downgraded her husband to David. She criticized Nabal and called him a fool. Instead of knowing where Abigail was, Nabal wanted to have a feast. Why was that? Was he aware that David was coming to kill him? Rather than having a plan to protect his house, wife, and servants, he had a social gathering. Perhaps he was conscious that this was his last night before dying, and he preferred to get drunk with wine rather than to ask for forgiveness or to spend his last moments on earth with his wife.

As Nabal was preparing to have a feast, Abigail was pleading for her life. There are several points to remember from her conversation with David. She had an action plan.

1. When she saw him, she fell on her face. That was a sign of worship and honor.
2. She opened her mouth at the right time and said, "My lord, bring iniquity on me. Let the blame be on me." She knew that a woman's punishment was different from a man's. Then, she asked for permission to speak. "I pray that you let me speak to you in front of this audience." She spoke in wisdom, "Listen to me, your handmaid. Please don't pay attention to Nabal, his name is foolish. As sure as the LORD lives, do not shed innocent blood; only deal with who wronged you."
3. She offered unto him a gift. "This gift that I present to you, let it be given to the young men who follow you."
4. Then she asked for mercy. "Will you please forgive me for trespassing? The LORD will make a sure house for my lord. You fight the battles of the LORD, and as the LORD protects you from your enemies, remember your handmaid."

David allowed her petition to be made known. She made her request, making sure things were secure for her. And when Nabal's life was spared, he had a heart attack or stroke; ten days later he died, leaving his house and wife unprotected.

She wasn't unprotected long. When David heard of Nabal's death, David said, "Blessed be the LORD, that has pleaded the cause of my reproach from the hand of Nabal, and kept his servant from evil: for the LORD has returned the wickedness of Nabal upon his own head. And David sent and communed with Abigail, to take her to be his wife" (1 Samuel 25:39KJV). Rather than getting a portion of Nabal's harvest, David got it all!

Men of excellence, don't let the Davids of this world snatch your wife from you because of a not too clever move in your attitude.

There is a time for all things. Well, this is the time to discover what your wife needs to keep her happy and at home.

When a woman leaves and you are not asked to come with her, your marriage is in serious trouble. What a woman is willing to leave will determine the outcome of the marriage between the two. Give her what you cannot find in another woman, and she will keep giving you whatever you want. All your needs will be met in her, your sweet and valuable wife.

CHAPTER 12

A Love So Strong

*L*ove is the spirit of the true expression of feelings and emotions which we share with another person. Love for a woman is like a small child who just received a new outfit on her birthday. She is pleased that her husband got the right color and style. To a man, love can be an opportunity to be Robbie Knieviel, who flies in the air on a motorcycle. Oh what joy! What a fantastic thrill it is to know that he beat the odds. He is able to make the scary jump. Love to a man can be the rush he gets when he makes it. Some skeptics say that it was easier for Robbie to make the jump than it was for his father, Evil Knieviel, to do it many years before. The fact remains, he did it.

Too, it doesn't matter how long it takes a man to fall in love. Finally he does, and he pours himself into the heart of a woman. He's relieved that he is able to trust a woman with his heart. He doesn't trust just any woman; his love is given to a strong woman who understands pain and rejection.

One who is healed from her wounds will not hurt another person. Wounded women and men hurt others. In fact, they will fight you on every hand. Even though you try to help, they are in serious discomfort. Your presence causes them to strike out with vengeance. Sometimes, it's best to let them bandage themselves. A wounded animal, especially a dog, will lick his own wounds and attempt to bite you if you make an effort to interfere. They think, like humans, that you are the enemy who is going to hurt them or take advantage, and their defense is to bite or hurt you. Back away until they are ready to receive you. Even though they made it through the pain, some still operate in pain. They overcame, but the thought of it remains.

HOLD HANDS AND WALK IN HIS GOODNESS

At this point, you have made the conscious decision either to remain in your marriage or to prepare for divorce. Before you make that move to divorce, give God another try. This is the time for you to move out of the way and let God do what He does.

From the bottom of your heart, you know that your relationship is different than anyone else's. Your love is strong, powerful, healthy, and stable. There may be a misunderstanding; things are out of order, but not enough to give up. You have to drown the voice of the adversary and not give up everything.

In front of you is an open door. Walk through it together. Can't you see the door? God is permitting your entrance. Hold hands and walk in His goodness, His grace, and His mercy. He doesn't want you to give up. He wants you to be as one.

In the Old Testament, there is a narrative about a man named Hosea and a woman called Gomer. She lived in the land of whoredom, and the Lord told him to love her and marry her. He obeyed God and married her. She had children who were not his children. Eventually, she left him, but his love was so strong that he later sought after her and bought her for fifteen pieces of silver and a homer and a half of barley.

Some theologians say, "He went and got her off the chopping block with silver and barley." Wherever she was, and by whatever means, he got her and said to her, "You must dwell as mine for many days. You shall not play the harlot or belong to another man. I will always be with you." That is a love so strong.

Why would God tell a man of God to go into the land of whoredom to marry a woman who would be unfaithful? Was there a message he was trying to convey? Yes, there was a serious message. Hosea loved Gomer. She loved him, but when life pressured her, she couldn't take it anymore. She ran back to what she knew and where she felt comfortable. But God said, "No. Life without me is impossible. The world can't have her."

God sent Hosea to get her back. He loved her so much that he forgot about the children she had from other men; he didn't dwell on her being a harlot. He wanted his wife, and he went after her.

Sometimes we have to be like Hosea to hear the voice of God and get our spouses back from the snare of the enemy. Forget about what they have done. Be grateful that they are still alive so you can tell them how you really feel without any outside negative forces.

I sense in my heart that God is telling someone to stay with a spouse, to reconnect, to sleep in the bed at the same time, to have breakfast and dinner together. Hold hands. Rub your feet, touching one another's feet as you would massage them in the sand.

Hosea and Gomer were used in comparison to the children of Israel. Israel blew it many times. God took them back after they cheated on Him. He took us back after we cheated on Him. We pretended we were happy; in actuality we were sad and disappointed with Him for many reasons. One relationship that we wanted to work crumbled. The job we really wanted was given to someone less qualified. We were disenchanted, and we didn't speak a word, nor did we voice our opinion to Him. We kept praising His name and reading the Word, but our actions told the truth. Even though we praised God and studied the Word, we were angry and we ran after other gods and bowed down before them. In some instances, we denied we were ever children of God. Not identifying who you are in Christ is a denial of Him.

You know what you did in anger when you attended the after work party. Going to the party wasn't the problem. The problem was when you smoked a cigar and took a martini. You were dying on the inside while you were being social and attempting to look good on the outside to keep another god contented. Afterward, you cried out for mercy. God being who He is treated us as He did the children of Israel. He had mercy upon us, and He took us back to be His people. And presently we say as they did, "Thou art my God."

UNCHAIN YOUR HEART

If God is your God, then your wife should be your wife or your husband should be your husband. Your life should not be turned upside down. If you are in, stay in. If you are out, remain out.

That punishment list of damaged feelings and emotions and what he or she should do to make up for the hurt and pain they caused must die. Suppose God is making a list and checking it twice of what we've done to Him. Where would we be, on or off the list?

A man may have longed after another woman's sweet smelling perfume, and a woman may have sought after another man's kind words and tender touch. But what drew you to your spouse? Whatever drew you together, give love permission to keep you from giving up on what you think is no longer alive.

Men of valor, your woman is kind in her attitude and in her words. But you are contemplating separation due to a past hurt that you can't release. Before you give up, give God another chance. He is the God of another chance. Unchain your heart, and accept love back into your marriage.

I believe beneath the hurt, love lives. Remember, my brother and sister, "love is not puffed up; it is not rude and it vaunts not itself. It is not easily provoked. But, love believes all things, bears all things, hopes all things, and endures all things" (1 Corinthians 13:4-5, 7 KJV).

Structure your marriage on the Lord, and both of you cry out, "Darling, love me into submission." Sweetly and gently I ask every woman who wants to be loved by her husband to be humble so he can rise above his circumstances and hold you tenderly in his arms, loving you with all that is within him.

I encourage every man to reflect on the good times and forget the bad times that pulled you away from the faith. I authorize you to wake up from your sleep. Be watchful, and strengthen the things which remain, that you be ready to die [crucify self] (Revelation 3:2), hold each other, and make passionate love.

LAY DOWN THE WEIGHT

Too many Christian couples want to divorce. What part of this process is the Word? In the Word, marriage is praiseworthy and respectful. Mister, if you think your wife was wrong for you, why has it taken fifteen or thirty years to find that you made a serious mistake? Your prayer should have been, "God, give me back the woman I married." Instead, you want to divorce her and marry someone else.

You can marry another woman. Remarry a woman who snores in your face every night. The thing is that you don't want to put forth an effort to get your wife back. You would rather pay child support and give her alimony. Somehow, you think you are being stretched, and it's too much pressure to stay home. For certain, you will be stretched, and it is for your good. Your marriage can go to another dimension. You have too much invested to let go. Perhaps you have seen the good, the bad, and the ugly in your wife. Take another look and see the good, the better, and the best. She is not the same woman you married. She became another woman, who changed as she raised your children and nurtured your heart and soul. She made sacrifices for you. She put her career on hold, taking odds jobs for your education. Lay down the weight, be obedient, and love your wife as Christ loved the church.

PICTURE YOUR LOVE

In January 2005, my husband was seriously ill. For days his feet were swollen, and they were getting larger. I was concerned that his body appeared swollen. He went to the VA doctor on a Friday, and he was told that he was all right. That report didn't set well in my spirit. The next morning, his entire body was swollen. Trying to convince a man to go to the doctor is tough, but to convince a man of God to go is a job only for the Almighty.

Late that evening, we called the paramedics. He was rushed to the local hospital. Twenty minutes after my arrival, I saw him on life support and heavily sedated. I asked the physician's assistant, "What happened to my husband? Why is he like that?"

He said, "We had to make him comfortable."

"Why?" I asked. He didn't have an answer, at least not one that I wanted to hear. He looked at me and walked away.

Several hours later, I saw a doctor and asked, "What is wrong with my husband?"

He said to me, "I will make him comfortable. We will do our best for him, until."

"Until what?" I asked.

He answered, "I won't be here tomorrow, but my staff will see to him."

I stated, "What is wrong with my husband? I have a ninety-four year old mother at home. I'm going to see her, and I will return."

Hurriedly I walked out of the hospital, trying urgently to get to my car. At first, I didn't quite understand what the doctor was saying, but as I walked to my car, it hit me like a hammer on my head that the doctor thought my darling husband was going to die. I yelled out, "The devil is a liar."

I immediately called our Pastor, Apostle T.C. Maxwell, and told him what was disclosed to me. He stated, "We will pray, and we are on our way." Subsequent to that statement, I don't remember what he said. I was crying; I knew he thought I was almost out of my mind.

After hanging up with him, I cried like a baby. My tears came because I thought the man I loved was leaving me for good, and I wasn't ready for our relationship to end. All I could dwell on was that I wanted him to touch me. I wanted us to make love, but we couldn't. Our last kiss had been two hours prior to the arrival of the paramedics. I needed a kiss, but that didn't happen. He remained in that state for approximately twenty-nine days. On the fourth day of his stay, two doctors asked me, "What do you recommend we do?"

I was startled. They were asking me, a non-medical professional, what to do. I gazed into their eyes and said, "You are the professionals; you tell me what your plans are. It has been four days, and he is not awake from the sedation. You told me it would take approximately twenty minutes. What must be done now?"

They had previously told me of a procedure to remove the fluid. I agreed! Anything, I thought, for him to rise from his bed of affliction. They reported to me that he had too much fluid on his lungs, and when the paramedics intubated him, they put the tube in wrong. The tube should have gone two inches below the esophagus, but it was stopped at the base of the esophagus and then clamped. That's why my husband was on life support. The procedure cut off his breathing. The doctors walked away in disbelief. I know they thought I was going to tell them to pull the plug. I had enough faith to know that my husband was going to make it. We would touch one another soon but in a greater pleasure.

Although Herb couldn't speak, gospel music and scriptures were played twenty-four hours, saturating his soul, mind, and spirit with the Word and affirmation of his deliverance. You may not be able to speak with your husband, but speak life to a dead situation and see God resurrect the dead. You may be told to let go, but don't you give up until you hear God say, "Give up, my daughter." Until then, do as I did. Anoint your home and his side of the bed, pray for him, and let the Word and Christian music play throughout your home, day and night. If you faint not, he will come back to be a better husband than he was before indulging in diverse types of sin.

Most of my time was spent at the hospital. From the hospital, I was moderating the church until his return. At home, I played music and prayed. In the end, with others praying for him, he rose from his bed. He left the hospital in a wheel chair, going to the rehabilitation center. He left there the Saturday before Easter (Resurrection Sunday), walking with a cane. I did not give up and allow the doctor to pull the plug. One doctor stated, "You need to face reality. The other doctors are not telling you the full truth. Your husband might die." In an anger moment, I strongly spoke, "The Lord has him covered, and you are also covered in the blood. God is not going to let anything happen to him, and the procedure you will do will not cause him to have a stroke or heart attack. You do what you must, and I'll do what I know best." He walked away from me angry, but I really didn't care about his negative behavior.

By faith, I knew Herb would overcome, and it was a matter of time for full recovery. For health care reasons, don't allow anyone to speak death to what you want to live. Move negative speakers out of your path.

That August, my ninety-four year old mother fell and broke her hip. We rushed her to Orange Park Medical City. One day, Herb's primary physician, Dr. Ogunfuwa, saw us; he stopped, rushed over, embraced Herb, and gave this testimony. "I don't know how your wife is at home. I didn't tell her this, but she didn't listen to us. She heard us, but by faith she stood on her belief and prayed for you. My faith was increased. She is a good woman."

With tears in Herb's eyes he said, "Thank you. She is a good woman." I am his good thing, which means at times being a good woman. I love my husband, and I feel this was my reasonable service. Day by day he is improving. We bless God that we had the fortitude, staying power, to give God and our marriage another chance.

DIVINE REVELATION

I had a celestial experience when Herb was in ICU. I wasn't asleep; I was resting. Early one morning, I saw an angel hovering over his hospital bed. The angel was dressed in a white gown, and I saw the glory cloud. I knew Herb was coming out soon.

When I got to the hospital, one of the nurses called me and said, "I don't mean to scare you, but I saw an angel dressed in white over your husband's bed."

I reached out and gave her a thankful hug. I said, "I saw the same thing about 5:30 a.m." She replied, "You are correct. That is what time it was."

Various pastors told me that Herb was in a coma. My response was, "No, he is resting in the presence of God. And he can hear you." Family members told me that he wasn't going to make it and that I should also face reality because his spirit was with God and his body was only a shell. Each time, I rebuked the devil, prayed, and worshipped God.

I refused the negative messages, but I heard every positive possibility of him coming out, in time, from resting in the Lord. As Prophetess A.R. Maxwell says, "He fasted for thirty days."

I wanted to hear healing not listen to the spirit of fear or doubt. We thank you, Prophetess, for giving me the healing scriptures.

The Lord strengthened me and held up my hand. Women, do what is right before the Lord. I realize that women of all ages send pleasing messages and dissatisfying messages to men without uttering a word. That technique is called non-verbal communication. Women can say a great deal without separating their lips.

Women love the touch. They will yield to a man. Yet on the subject of submission, they will silently ask, "Why is it necessary to submit to a man? To whom does he submit? Why is there so much pressure and responsibility on the woman submitting?"

Just for those who speak from their expressions, I wrote these words.

I've surrendered my life to Christ, the author and finisher of my faith, but I will not submit to you until you know who you are and who I am to you! You are uncertain of what you have. I am a precious jewel given to you by God. He was awesome in His creation of man, yet He was majesty as He took man's rib and made woman for compatibility. I was made for you! I was made to love, cherish, honor, respect, and make you feel fantastic at all times. Allow the tenderness of you to come forth in me so that I can hold you in my arms, embracing the one who called me woman and saw that I was bone of his bones and flesh of his flesh. Call me softly; I am your woman, for I came from you. Touch me tenderly with your emotions! When you are uncertain about the gift you have and the value of it, never misuse me. But go back to the Creator in humility. He will reaffirm what you have, and then you will know that I humbly surrender myself to you. I have been waiting to succumb to the man I adore and admire. We can behold the beauty of holiness and the beauty of ecstasy together. Darling, I submit my life to you.

Hold on to those words and grab that man. Contrary to popular opinions, a woman will follow a man who has a dream or a vision. She will not follow someone who has no clue of his future. She knows that without a vision there is division. The same principle applies to the church. Where there is not vision, the people perish

(Proverbs 29:18). Divine revelation! Just as man follows God, a woman follows a man. If he falls and pulls completely away from God, he leaves her to follow God alone.

As a man separates from God, he may make decisions that are not in agreement with God's thinking. Without God's presence, he loses power and has no voice in the home. Don't get me wrong, women are not being downplayed. We enjoy being alone with God, building a more excellent relationship. We are intelligent and capable decision makers. But we don't need that burden on us when man and woman can contribute together. Women really love a strong man who is sensitive. Regardless of his Christian walk, if he makes sound decisions, she will submit.

Great revelation has come across the pulpit on women understanding submission. Great men and women preachers have learned to use wisdom before articulating the message of submission. They never want a woman to have a sour expression on her face before the Scripture is ever read, which reads, "You must be crazy. I submit." Also, those preachers didn't want women to reach into their handbags, pull out a stick of gum, cross their arms and legs, and chew gum diligently before the principal message was given.

Some leaders have observed just that. If a woman reached into her handbag to take out a stick of gum, there was nothing they could tell her. As far as the woman was concerned, the sermon was concluded and all the preacher needed to do was close the Bible, pray a short prayer, and dismiss.

I'll assure you that there are still women who don't want to hear a message on submission. They are tired of hearing that message. Women get queasy hearing what they should do considering what the man has not done.

My thoughts on the matter were that women didn't understand the full meaning of this misunderstood word, because it had the tendency to discourage hearts and create wrath within the home and in the church. If women felt it was a negative word, nothing positive could possibly be received in their spirit to change their belief system. My prayer is for God to give me divine revelation to reach the heart of women for a breakthrough in this area. It is not a difficult process, but without a good understanding of the word, it can become an issue.

I have learned that submission is an act of trust. Trust therefore is defined as having confidence, commitment, and total honesty with a person. When we trust someone, we open our hearts and become vulnerable. It doesn't matter if you are male or female; you'll empty yourselves into that person.

LIE UNDER HIM SUBMISSIVELY

Put yourself in position and just submit. Submit to him in a humble manner. Everything is going to be all right. So what if he doesn't attend church? He lets you go! You knew he wasn't saved before your marriage, and you accepted him. Why the change? It was obvious that he was going to be a good provider, and you gave in for the finances and whatever else.

As the weaker vessel, it is an honor to fall under Herb. So often our husbands wrap their bodies around us in the moment of ecstasy, and we lie under them submissively and willingly without a complaint. Near a warm fire on a winter evening, we are resting our heads in their laps as they caress our hair. My goodness, it is a fantastic thought to be under them as they demonstrate affection. What a wonderful feeling it is to submit to them through the power of love and devotion! Walk in the sense of humbleness. Humbleness is a state of lowliness and meekness. Submission is not degrading! If anything, it is being under him, getting out of the way of the force that's about to come.

WISDOM IN LIVING UNDER HIM

As a single woman, I was close to my children, mother, and brothers. There wasn't a man in my life. There had been several men who infrequently came to see me. They came because they thought I was in need of companionship. But I wasn't, and they didn't matter to me. As I spoke to them with authority that I was contented in my heart and that I was waiting for my husband, some of them spoke negatively saying that I wasn't qualified to preserve myself until that special man came. I must confess, I've made many mistakes in life. I fell down on numerous occasions, but I got up. And I was free to communicate that I didn't need them. I'd been made free and was free indeed (John 8:36).

I was more determined than ever to wait on my husband. I began to prepare for him. As I confessed and called my husband into existence, doubt overshadowed me at times, but I knew marriage was for me.

There I was, thirty-two and thinking marriage wasn't coming fast enough. In addition to that, I had three sons, and even though I was waiting for my husband, no one was interested in marrying a woman with three mouths to feed. I almost gave up on my confessions.

Despite those thoughts, I continued to make that prophetic announcement that I was going to be married by the time I was thirty-four years of age. My family laughed. Guess what? In the end I laughed the loudest. On April 4, 1981, Herb and I became one. The day after, our journey began.

Ministers of the gospel told us that we were not compatible and our marriage was not going to last. They also said that he would never be successful as a pastor until he walked out of my life. His co-workers asked, "Why her? You could have done better." Many were intimidated by my presence. I didn't understand why. They didn't know me. They only knew that I wasn't good enough for him.

Many fiery darts were sent to us, aimed at me. I thank God for teaching me the wisdom of living under my husband, where I could pray while Herb protected me from any harm and danger. If I had given up and walked out of his life, I couldn't tell you effectively to stay with your husband or with your wife and build a successful marriage.

Too many have given up on God and have walked away from their marriages before God made the change. They see the manifestation of their prayers, but the results are with someone else. The new husband is enjoying your prayers for a submissive wife. The new wife loves your ex-husband, who was a drunk but who is now sober and in ministry. You threw the clock down, but another person kept praying. The clock kept ticking, and in walked your former wife or husband.

I WAS TEMPTED

It was in my mind that Herb was going to leave me for ministry. He was pressured by others to divorce me or separate from me. They thought that he would succeed in ministry if he left me. I was tempted to give them what they wanted, but the Holy Spirit told me to call back my love towards my husband to defeat the negative bits and pieces that were sent out into the atmosphere to kill our love. The devil was a liar.

The Holy Spirit drove the demonic forces from our lives. While we were healing, my heart told me to continue in the relationship, but my mind told me that I could do better. Guess what, I held on to my husband. I told the devil that he could not have him. I went into spiritual warfare to save my marriage. I fasted and prayed and made passionate love to my husband.

Before the miracle, we almost became that couple in chapter 4. While I changed my mind I didn't renounce it in my spirit. It is important that a spiritual cleansing is completed and every ounce of residue has left your mind, soul and spirit. If not, at an inopportune moment, that specific thing will return to pursue you. Bishop and I were blessed beyond measures. We analyzed the stormy waves of the sea, and survived the marriage. It was a difficult fight, but we made it. All our needs were placed in God's hand. He supplied what we needed to make it.

You must remember that the LORD will fight for you; you need only to be still (Exodus 14:14 NIV). I had to be still and ask God to change me. I knew if my environment changed, we would return to that place in God with body, soul, and spirit. I was determined that I wasn't going to lose another husband to a circumstance, to another woman, to the lack of finance, or for whatever reason. It wasn't going to happen. By any means necessary, my marriage would be saved.

With a mind to stand still and a heart of faith, our marriage was healed. My husband, knowing that I was his good thing, had to find me in position with God. He found me twenty-five years ago, and I'm glad. We embraced each other, and we are contented and satisfied in our state.

CHAPTER 13

Darling, Love Me Into Submission

*S*ubmission is conquered as you give or release power and control over to another person. Submission really has to do with to whom we open our hearts: a good man or an evil man. My objective is to get negativity out of the home and to bring healing to both spouses. It may be difficult, but I need your help. We know that there are women who demonstrate submission unto God, whom they have not seen, but are unable to humble themselves to their own husbands.

Down through the years, I have listened to women speak words of this nature, "As soon as he treats me right, I will respect him. When he earns respect I will give it. Until he does what he promised, I will not submit to him. I won't submit to a man who is not saved. He needs to keep a job before I submit."

Does this sound like somebody you know? It is amazing how we find it so easy to submit to God, a dear friend, a supervisor, and a pastor without hesitation. But it aggravates our hearts to submit to our spouses. Why is it difficult to submit? If we were to examine the word submission, most women would gladly appreciate the fact that it is a good thing to submit to their own husbands.

It is a good thing to submit. After all, "the head of every man is Christ, and the head of the woman is man, and the head of Christ is God" (1 Corinthians 11:3). As man is the head of the woman, he has the responsibility of taking care of the woman and protecting her. As the head, fiery darts come to him, not to you. As you submit, you are under him, beneath him, praying for God's guidance and direction for your husband to get clarity as he provides for you.

This proves to us that we must be one in the Spirit and one in the body, believing that Christ is one with the Father. Jesus said in John 17,

> But now I come to you; and these things I speak in the world so that they may have My joy made full in themselves. I have given them Your word; and the world has hated them, because they are not of the world, even as I am not of the world. I do not ask You to take them out of the world, but to keep them from the evil one. They are not of the world, even as I am not of the world. Sanctify them in the truth; Your word is truth. As You sent Me into the world, I also have sent them into the world. For their sakes I sanctify Myself, that they themselves also may be sanctified in truth. I do not ask on behalf of these alone, but for those also who believe in Me through their word; that they may all be one; even as You, Father, are in Me and I in You, that they also may be in Us, so that the world may believe that You sent Me. The glory which You have given Me I have given to them, that they may be one, just as We are one; I in them and You in Me, that they may be perfected in unity, so that the world may know that You sent Me, and loved them, even as You have loved Me. Father, I desire that they also, whom You have given Me, be with Me where I am, so that they may see My glory which You have given Me, for You loved Me before the foundation of the world. O Righteous Father, although the world has not known You, yet I have known You; and these have known that You sent Me; and I have

made Your name known to them, and will make it known, so that the love with which You loved Me may be in them, and I in them.

John 17:12-26

We are one in Christ, as He and the Father are one. Therefore, we have a right to submit to our husbands, as Christ submits to his Father. This may be difficult for a woman who doesn't know Christ to understand. But to a woman who knows Him, this must come automatically. You can't introduce non-Christians to Christ before you introduce them to your husband, your lord, protector, guide, and director. If the home is not in order, it is my belief that we can hinder the church from operating decently and in order. The Bible encourages us to "Let all things be done decently and in order" (1 Corinthians 14:40). God does things decently and in order.

Jesus told those who were assigned to Him about the Father. Then, He demonstrated how He was submissive to the Father. The principal thing is to do as Christ did. Obey and submit to our heavenly Father. Likewise wives, submit as Christ submitted to the Father. Do as he did. We are to pattern ourselves after Christ. Adorn yourselves with submission to your husbands.

Every woman wants to hear her husband say, "You are a wonderful wife. I adore you, and I can't do anything without you. You give me great joy. You are a fantastic mother. You include me in your plans, and even when you're tired, you rest in my arms. You are concerned about me, and I really do appreciate you for being my wife."

After hearing such words, a wife wants her husband to kiss her on her cheek or hold her in his arms. Some husbands may not be affectionate as far as touching and caressing a wife's body. They are good with words. Therefore, they caress with wonderful words. We love to hear words from our husband's lips. Therefore, his touch is not that important. Really, it isn't. A wife wants her husband to speak from his heart words that will enthrall her soul.

What is important is that a wife's listening will change the no touch behavior. She doesn't have to stress over that. There is no set rule which states you can't touch him. He doesn't have to touch you; you can make a move on him. He's your man! Touch his mind with a soft stroke that brings chills down his spine. Kiss his lips gently, look in his eyes, squeeze his buttocks, and watch carefully as he opens his eyes with unexpected enchantment to touch you with a pat of romanticism.

It didn't matter how I longed for Herb to touch me, he couldn't. Therefore, I reached out and touched him; soothingly rubbing his skin was an honor. It was a privilege anointing his feet with oil and praying over his body. Embracing one another was out of sight for a moment. His precious touch that used to shake my heart and made my body succumb was placed on hold temporarily. That was a temporary circumstance, which did not mean we were not going to touch or caress again. The past touch from his hands is no longer present, but the new touch makes me feel as if I can leap tall buildings. His touch is soft and innocent; it is no longer polluted. The old man died to his past, and the new man thinks only of me, my beauty, and my devotion to him.

The touches from your man shook your heart once and made your body succumb; give him the opportunity to touch you. As he touches you, surrender and tell him what you need. Forget the frustration. Picture your love, and let it flow through your mind until it chills your body. Boldly yet gently speak, "My darling husband, not only do I want you to make love to me, I need you to love me unconditionally. With that love should come respect from your heart, embracing me with words of softness, reassuring me that in my weakness you become my strength and that in my inadequacies, you will lift me up in prayer that I gain wisdom from God. I need you desperately to love me with your mind, soul, and spirit. Sweetheart, you must rescue me from all emotional temptations with the sweet sounding words that come softly from your lips. Seriously, there is an ultimate need to know that you are with me. Honey, love me as you love yourself. Take care of me as you care for yourself. I know that your voice is strong and powerful because our Creator's voice is strong and powerful, and it is full of majesty. As I give unto the Lord the glory that's due Him, I am in right standing with you to give honor and to reverence your name. As I worship the Lord in the beauty of holiness (Psalm 29:2, 4), I worship you in spirit and in truth (John 4:24). Hold me in the tenderness of your arms. I love being in your presence. I will lay my life down for you because I sense in my spirit that you'll lay down your life for me" (1 John 3:16).

WE ARE APPRECIATIVE OF ANOTHER DAY

I wanted another chance to touch Herb and to articulate my affections. The God we serve woke my man from his sleep, and we speak precious words to each other. We are appreciative of another day to thank God for life, marriage, health, and strength. We are together! We are enjoying happiness in the state of oneness.

LORD, KING, AND PRIEST

Before Herb's illness, I saw him as my lord, king, and priest. I've discovered that submission is an awesome weapon. It allows him to know without doubt that he can trust me with his heart, knowing that I will not discredit him no matter what is happening in our relationship. Your husband needs to know that as you submit, power is a representation of your strength and you have the ability to do above whatever you ask or think to make him feel like the lord, king, and priest of his home.

HE GIVES BACK TO YOU

He knows that you are sober-minded, well disciplined, temperate, kind-hearted, and willing to be subordinate to him. He knows that you love him and will take care of your children.

He gives back to you loving words that are brief and pointed. "Honey, I left my father and mother to cleave to you. You are my noonday strength; you give me insight on ordinary things. The words that proceed from your lips are gentle and powerful. You are loyal to me, and I appreciate you for not giving up. You hardly notice any of my faults. Thank you for working with me to keep our marriage together."

LONG LIFE OF MUTUAL LOVE

Marriage is an intimate relationship between man and woman. God ordains the bed for man and woman to enjoy sex, so don't let age and old traditions destroy your marriage by not engaging in sexual socialization. This is what makes a healthy marriage, demonstrating your love to each other. Don't let the enemy cut a wedge between you. If this happens, your man will withdraw. You should be willing to open up to him with your sweet smelling perfume and live a long life of mutual love.

THE REAL LOVEMAKING

Yearn for your man; keep him on your heart. Communicate with him. Communication is important in a marriage. Never assume that you know each other and that you can read him or her like a book. Sometimes, when the book is reread, you find something that was overlooked or ignored. Spend time learning each other, and never take each other for granted. Usually, when a spouse is taken for granted, there is no room for creativity. My sister, don't you dare give up. Look fervently from your heart, and find your man. When he is found, embrace him in your arms; bring him home.

Sometimes, we get used to seeing one another and we take our spouses for granted. The morning breakfast in bed disappears. His lying in your lap stops. Going shopping together is out of the question. Sharing chores is an assignment for you only and not his responsibility. Take a look at where you are and the things that are missing.

Do what you must to get the joy back. Get the real lovemaking together, not the little quickies. You are not a quickie woman. He should take time to romance you. Wake up and smell the roses! You are unable to smell them if there aren't any. But you can buy some, and not the daisies. Meanwhile, put on a pot of coffee. As it brews, smell it before you are singing, "Good night lonely heart, my man has gone."

SAVE YOUR MARRIAGE

With skillful communication you can save your marriage. Save your marriage by giving up pride. It is obvious that you love him and he loves you. You live in the house together, but you live separate lives. You cannot tell me that this arrangement is settled in your spirit. I don't think so. Stop lying to yourselves, and move forward. Destroy the yokes that are preventing you from living in harmony.

As I mentioned earlier, if you can praise and reverence God whom you have not seen, you surely can honor and adore your spouse. When you really submit to Christ as being the head of the church, you will submit to your husband. He is the head of the wife. You can do it. You are constantly convincing other women to let no corrupt communication proceed out of their mouths. Now it's time for you to practice what you preach, a sermon in humility. "Let all bitterness, and wrath, and anger, and clamor, and evil speaking, be put away from you, with all malice: and be kind one to another, tenderhearted, forgiving one another, even as God for Christ's sake has forgiven you" (Ephesians 4:31-32 KJV).

CHAPTER 14

Love, Honor, and Respect

oth spouses, who have not reached the realm of humility, should take a sober look at themselves to see whether they need to let go of their independent status or their self-determination of authority to have control.

In their minds they should be thinking, "Honey, since I met you my life is happier than ever before. Before you, my heart was broken into many small pieces. I had no direction, but you gave me hope, hope to recognize that I am worth something. I didn't realize I had potential until I met you. Always you encouraged me to walk in victory. I overcame many things; you helped to usher me into spending precious moments with God. My faithfulness in God is strong as you carried me until I was able to enter into His presence. Now that I am matured and have grown tremendously in God, we can hold hands in the spirit, move obstacles, speak to the mountains, and they shall be removed."

In a marriage where there is forced liberty or freedom, the devil has control of the family and the home. Somewhere the head of the household has allowed the enemy to come in and separate the rich, powerful love that they once had. Now they are operating independently, alone, but thinking that because they are in the same house they are together. This is not so! You are seriously apart, and the devil knows he has power and control over you. You relinquished what God gave to you from the beginning. Go back and get it.

He created you in His image, with power, authority and strength. You need to take back what you gave the devil and what he snatched out of your hand. We all made mistakes, and God has forgiven us. It is time for us to forgive others. We should be on our knees praying that God restore what we forfeited out of ignorance, jealousy, and stupidity.

In your marriage, one is capable of more help than the other. One is mature, and the other is immature. The behavior that is more dormant is wrecking the marriage. Or else, it could be the less dormant one who is blocking progress. You need help! Cry out and ask for it. "Our help is in the name of the LORD, who made heaven and earth" (Psalm 124:8).

Cry out to the Lord that you submit to hearing your spouse's voice, seeing his or her smile, and enjoying a lovely kiss. Out of the depths of despair, cry unto the Lord and ask Him to hear your voice and to let His ears be attentive to the voice of your supplication. Your soul waits for the Lord more than they that watch for the morning. With the Lord there is mercy and plenty of redemption (Psalm 130:1-2, 6-7).

In Donald E. Moore's book, *A Daily Guide to a Better Marriage*, he stated, "We must understand that our marriage partner is not perfect, cannot be, and will never be perfect. Don't try to make your companion live up to a standard that he or she can never reach; after all, you are not perfect either. When a person becomes angry or confused, he has a tendency to try to force or drive, rather than lead with love. You may be trying to force your mate into changing instead of loving him or her into changing. I find that most people spend more time complaining than helping. If you will be honest with yourself, you may find that you are complaining all the time about what your mate is doing wrong, instead of helping him or her to do it right. Many times we find ourselves spending more time helping strangers than we do our own family, You must take time to work with your own loved ones. Take time to teach and help each other. Even ministers fall into this trap. A pastor may help or teach others, but does he take the time to minister to his own wife or children? In dealing with others, we must remember that a right attitude often makes the difference between success and failure. People can feel what come from your spirit, whether good or bad, love or hate. Think before you speak. Is what you are about to say to your mate a fitly spoken word? Is it in the right attitude? What you say, and how you say it, may well determine whether you convince your mate you are sincerely trying to help him or her to overcome a weakness."[5]

Think before you speak. Use wisdom! Ask God for wisdom, knowledge and understanding. He continued with, "For a real breakthrough to come in your marriage, you must learn to forgive and to forget your entire partner's past failures and mistakes. We sometimes find this hard to do because there are some things we simply don't want to forgive and forget. Somewhere we have gotten the mistaken idea that we need to hold on to our mate's past failures and mistakes to use as a weapon against him or her in time of argument. No marriage will ever succeed until the partners learn to forgive as Christ forgave. How did He forgive? He forgave – and forgot! Remember, 'Love never fails.' The weapon with which you are going to win the battle is not a carnal or fleshly weapon, but rather it is with love that you win the victory."[6]

After reading this book, let your partner love on you. Give them the opportunity to caress you. They will not take advantage of you anymore. Those days are long gone. They saw that your heart is the seat of love (1Timothy 1:5). They have changed from their old ways. Believe it or not, they now trust in God, who raised Christ from the dead. Your faith and hope can rest in Christ.

You can also release your mind to have real love for everyone because your soul has been cleansed from selfishness and hatred

5 Donald E. Moore, A daily guide to a Better marriage (Harrison House, Inc.: Tulsa, Oklahoma, 1983) p. 3-6
6 Moore, p 8

when you trusted Christ to save you. So see to it that you really do love each other warmly, with all your hearts (1 Peter 1:2-25 TLB).

You have a new life. It was not passed on to you from your parents, for the life they gave you will fade away. This new one will last forever, for it comes from Christ, God's ever-living message to men. Yes, our natural lives will fade as grass does when it becomes brown and dry. All our greatness is like a flower that droops and falls; but the Word of the Lord will last forever. And his message is the Good News that was preached to you (1 Peter 1:23-25 TLB).

Give in and grow in the power of the Lord. It's not by might or by power that you do this, but it's by Christ's Spirit. Commit to your husbands. Men, surrender your love to your wives.

Commitment is a choice. You made the decision to commit to God. Now make the choice to get your life in order and do those things according to the precepts and statures of God.

If you are a follower of Jesus Christ, you must do as He did. He followed the Father in trust. You will trust Him, obey Him, and commit unto Him, or you will deny Him and do things your way. To be a follower of Christ Jesus, you must trust and have confidence in Him.

Jesus said to his disciples, "If anyone desires to come after Me, let him deny himself, and take up his cross and follow me" (Matthew 16:24).

Take up the cross of disobedience, pride, arrogance, un-forgiveness, jealousy, hatred, and pain. Give it to Jesus. Whatever you give to Him will no longer be remembered. Forget and forgive! Let go of all of it. It's God's plan for man and woman to commit to each other in love and with deep devotion.

Go! Get your wife, and cuddle her with your love. You have been raised from the dead. Life everlasting is in your marriage! Jesus has quickened the dead and called forth those things that do not exist as if they did (Romans 4:17). The Lord God is your strength (Habakkuk 3:19).

Submit to your husband when he comes to you in a humble manner. When his arms are outstretched, walk into them. Take him into your arms, hold him, comfort him, admire and adore his greatness and his loving kindness.

At last, be of one mind, having compassion one for another. Be courteous, kind, and gentle. As you obey and serve each other, you will have good success and eat the good of the land.

In wanting a submissive marriage, bear in mind that love is kind. Be kind in your attitude with words. "Love is not rude and it vaunts not itself, is not puffed up. It is not easily provoked. But, love bears all things, believes all things, hopes all things, and endures all things" (1 Corinthians 13:4-5, 7). Assemble your marriage on the Lord, and both of you can cry out, "Where love, honor, and respect dwell, we are loved into submission."

This Is Not the End, Only Your Beginning!

Bibliography

Munroe, Myles. <u>Single, Married, Separated, and Life After Divorce.</u> Destiny Image, Inc: Shippensburg, PA., 1989

Moore, Donald E. <u>A Daily Guide to a Better Marriage.</u> Harrison House, Inc.: Tulsa, Oklahoma, 1983

McCormick, Eugene, Dr.. "Single Life: Fulfillment in the Word," Temple of Light Fellowship Ministries, Jacksonville, Florida, 25 March 2006